OUT OF THE BOX LEARNING

EMPOWERING **YOU** ON YOUR HOMESCHOOL JOURNEY

Beverly Burgess

Out of the Box Learning
Empowering **YOU** on Your Homeschool Journey

By
Beverly Burgess

Out of the Box Learning: Empowering YOU on Your Homeschool Journey
Copyright © 2016 Beverly Burgess. Produced and printed by Stillwater River Publications. All rights reserved. Written and produced in the United States of America. This book may not be reproduced or sold in any form without the expressed, written permission of the authors and publisher.

Visit our website at **www.StillwaterPress.com** for more information.

First Stillwater River Publications Edition

ISBN-10: 0-997-8778-7-1
ISBN-13: 978-0-997-8778-7-8

Library of Congress Control Number: 2016958522

1 2 3 4 5 6 7 8 9 10
Written by Beverly Burgess
Cover Design by Dawn M. Porter
Published by Stillwater River Publications, Glocester, RI, USA.

Publisher's Cataloging-In-Publication Data
(Prepared by The Donohue Group, Inc.)

Names: Burgess, Beverly, 1968-
Title: Out of the box learning : empowering you on your homeschool journey / by Beverly Burgess.
Description: First Stillwater River Publications edition. | Glocester, RI, USA : Stillwater River Publications, [2016]
Identifiers: LCCN 2016958522 | ISBN 978-0-9978778-7-8 | ISBN 0-9978778-7-1
Subjects: LCSH: Burgess, Beverly--Family. | Home schooling. | Learning disabled children--Education. | Education--Parent participation. | Alternative education.
Classification: LCC LC40 .B87 2016 | DDC 371.04/2--dc23

The views and opinions expressed in this book are solely those of the author and do not necessarily reflect the views and opinions of the publisher.

Acknowledgements

My heartfelt thanks to my husband of 26 years, Larry. Your unwavering support, confidence, and love get me through every single day. To my three amazingly weird and wild children, you are the heart and soul of this book. Many thanks to my homeschool community for always uplifting me, and showing me new and unimaginable things and ways of learning. My father who passed away in 2004, taught me many life's lessons and I carry them through every page of this book.

I am blessed beyond imagination living out of the box.

Let your deepest fears be your launching pad

for your greatest calling.

~Anonymous

Contents

Part 1 The Personal 1

    Tomatoes 3

    Beginnings 7

    Trusting Your Gut 9

    Butterflies 19

    Unsettled 23

    Enough 34

    Endings 41

    Decisions 62

    The Summer of Transition 68

    Homeschool Groups & Family Ties 77

    Special Needs 79

Part II The Practical 87

    You Can Homeschool 89

    Homeschooling and Public School 97

    Educationese 101

    Why Homeschool? 104

    The Marriage Dance, Self-Care & the Mess 107

    The S Word 112

    The Honeymoon Phase & Deschooling 117

    The Naysayers 121

    Homeschooling Mistakes 128

    State Homeschooling Requirements & Your Role ...132

    Homeschool Groups & Cooperatives 135

Learning Styles 140
The Ideal Homeschool...146
Homeschooling Through Illness..148
Getting Through the Hard Days 151
Homeschooling While Working..154
Organizing Your Homeschool Space 157
Curriculum Searching..165
Homeschooling Multiple Grades & Ages 173
Planning the Full Year...176
Lesson Plans 181
Determining Progress 187
Alternate Ways to Learn...195
The Highschool Years 197
Closing..227
Epilogue..229

Introduction

"We need to move beyond the idea that education is something provided for us, and toward the idea that an education is something that we create for ourselves."

~Stephen Downes

There is not much more I enjoy than being organized and planning. It delights and thrills me to come up with a grand scheme of master mindedness and have it play out completely as intended. Every dot adhered to, every T crossed, every line filled in perfectly. If only things would go as planned.

Most days, I wonder why I plan at all, and other days I wonder if I planned enough. But the "if onlys" always get you. If only one more detail was in place, if only the bus weren't late, if only I took the extra step, if only they had listened to me. If only.

From a complicated childhood to a messy childbirth to a muddled education for my kids, — everything and every detail in my life was planned accordingly. Only, what I had planned and what the universe thought should happen, were two very different things.

Life has a way of saying, "Uh-uh, that is not the plan. Do it this way."

Planning has both helped me, and held me hostage at times. Planners, like me, have expected outcomes, and those outcomes help us to feel safe and secure. I made a good plan, therefore the outcome should be written as prescribed. Right? But that wasn't the case in my child's public school education. While public school was well planned, the outcome was disastrous, and by no means, did it make anyone in our family feel safe and secure.

One would think after so many times of life getting in the way of my ultimate plan, that I would learn to go with the flow a bit more. Indeed, it was a lesson I learned in my mid-thirties when I began homeschooling my kids. But, well laid plans get derailed in the most marvelous and in the most heart wrenching of ways. We can either find the lessons from what the universe teaches us — and grow, or we can wallow in self-pity that things didn't turn out as we planned. My father taught me to look for the lessons, and that defeatism got you nowhere. If you don't like what the universe offered up to you, you and only you are responsible for changing it.

To some, homeschooling may seem like an educational choice too far outside the box of a typical education. For others like myself, it has been a time of empowerment, and learning to trust myself and my children. You cannot separate homeschooling from the person or family that is doing it. It is more than a new way to learn, it is a way to live your values and rethink education for all children.

Learning is messy work. It was for my son Patrick, and then for my other two children, and should be messy for every child. Learning requires muddy hands, and dirty fingernails and asking questions. Learning is not a straight road through certain grades, at certain times once one has absorbed all the knowledge that is mandated. It is a winding path, an ebb and flow that is forever changing.

Once I started homeschooling, the old myths and hearsay began to fall to the wayside. I explored NHERI, the National Home

Education Resource Institute (www.nheri.com) and was surprised to learn that;

- Home-educated students score in the 65-80th percentile on national standardized achievement tests. This is 15-30 points higher than public schooled children.
- Home-educated students score above average regardless of whether either parent has a teaching certificate or college degree.
- There is no correlation between the degree of state regulation or control over homeschooling and homeschool achievement. Homeschooled children in states with little or low regulation do just as well on all testing, as those in high regulation states.
- Home-educated students are more engaged in their communities including civic activities like voting, sports teams, church activities and community service.
- Homeschooled children frequently interact with a wider variety of people of all ages and not just same-aged peers.

My children challenged me endlessly on this journey; Patrick in particular, because without him, we would never have begun homeschooling. My firstborn, in a sense, forced me to find new ways and methods of learning, that were unlike anything offered to us before.

My first tentative steps into homeschooling were not easy. Homeschooling made me uncomfortable because everything I knew learning to be, started to be replaced with new thoughts, ideas, and new philosophies; as well as a deep trust that my children were inherent learners. Everything I thought I knew about learning and education began to unravel, as it tested my old ideals. I would equate the experience with losing one's religion, where you can no longer align your beliefs with what has been taught to you your entire life.

Beverly Burgess

    I hope this book makes you uncomfortable too, and that it challenges your beliefs and ideals about education. I hope you plow your own path in homeschooling, and rejoice in the freedom and the pure love of learning.

Part 1 The Personal

Tomatoes

On a hazy evening of summer, I watched my father's silhouette move up and down the aisles of the garden bed. The heat from the day hung heavily as foggy puffs of clouds formed around his ankles. Behind him, the sky exploded in fiery reds and golds, and then just as quickly, softened to the delicate pinks and grays of a watercolor. The garden stakes, lined up like soldiers in the night, kept their guard watch over the growing troops. Dad huffed as he moved his way along the base of every plant, fingering each seedling. His cool breath disturbed the warm air in big lifts of energy-filled exhales, that distorted the glow of the summer sunset in big whorls and orbs.

In daylight, Dad was an imposing man. But tonight in the fading light, his outline didn't match what I knew to be true about him. Years of heavy smoking and drinking had given him the predictable beer gut and muscle wasting, and his shadow gave away all of his secrets.

Making his way down to the end of the row of tomatoes, Dad stood up; his blackened framework in sharp contrast to the colors surrounding him. His bulbous knees seemed incapable of supporting his mammoth belly sitting atop his Bermuda shorts. With his protruding abdomen and tiny waist cinched up by his belt, his profile was cartoonish.

    I watched his nostrils flare as the bending, and reaching, and pulling of weeds tired him, and caused his lungs to protest. With one hand on his hip and the other resting on his pregnant belly, he looked over his work in the fading light and exhaled through his teeth.

    "You gotta plant the tomatoes a little sideways, in the deepest hole you can dig — it makes stronger roots," he yelled to me down at the end of the row. His smoker's cough and booming voice startled me from my evening firefly hunt. I inched closer to him, not quite sure if he was asking me to help him, or if he planned to impart some gardening wisdom on me.

    "When those tomatoes get top-heavy, you need some strong roots to hold them up," he added. I stepped by his side and could smell his summer sweat with each reach of his arms. "Don't make much difference if you got the biggest and best tomatoes and nothin' to help keep them rooted in what they know. Put a fish head in each hole, and if you don't have that, add a little Epsom salt — it helps balance everything the tomato needs. Balance is the key — not too much of any one thing. There ain't much that can go wrong unless Mother Nature decides to be a bitch and drown us in her tears, or unless she creates a dust bowl. Too much rain and the tomatoes rot before they ripen. Not enough rain and they won't have anything in them that makes them a tomato. And don't be so quick to prune off the leaves right from the get-go. Them leaves are like an umbrella on the beach: sun still gets through but you don't get blisters on the skin. Gotta let the light in but only when it's time," he said.

    "Hose water won't help you much either, even in a drought. Them garden plants need rainwater, straight from the sky, and they need it good and steady and on a regular basis. Sure as coffee in the morning and supper on the table each night. If God don't see fit to make it a good year, all the work you do will be for nothin'. Can't control what's out of your hands anyway — no use tryin'," he said.

Dad plucked a big hornworm from the tomato plant and squished it between his fingers; the green innards seeping down his hand and dripping to the ground below. He flicked away the extra bits of guts from his fingernails. "Be sure to pinch out the suckers and anything the tomato don't need — they drain too much energy from the plant. Plants can only do one thing at a time, just like people. If you focus on that one thing, and then move on to the next thing — then you got it figured out," he told me.

"Mmm-hmmm," I answered. "But, what if you don't know how to do that one thing, or don't even know what that one thing is?" I asked.

Dad sat for a while on the turned-over bucket, coughed and said, "Well, then you got to get real quiet and sit with it, and listen to what that voice inside you is sayin'. People gotta listen more to that voice inside them — it's usually right. Sometimes it's just a whisper, and sometimes it's loud as thunder. You have to pay attention to the big and little things, and make sure you ain't changing the story in your head, to fit what you want to happen. Bottom line is all things need a chance. Sometimes it gets done right the first time. Sometimes it means givin' 'em a little more time to catch up, and sometimes it means weeding out things that don't work. The trick is knowing when."

"But, how do you know when is the right time?" I groaned.

Dad swung his pencil-thin legs over the end of the row of eggplants and pulled out a spindly looking growth with brown leaves. "See," he said. "That right there needs to go. Just like a runt in a litter of pigs or a weakling plant in a garden, if you gave it some time and it still can't figure out what it's supposed to do, you gotta help it make the only choice it can. You gotta let go of what don't work."

The gnats were starting to swarm as the last light of the evening disappeared. Dad yanked a hunk of lemon balm from the garden and began swatting his exposed skin, inoculating himself with a veil of lemony citrus that the gnats didn't dare to cross. Mom turned on the back porch light and the moths started to gather for their evening fire dance.

Dad handed me the bucket with the garden waste spilling over the sides, and I crammed my foot down deep inside the tin to compact them down.

"Give them weeds to the guinea hens," he said.

"Even weeds got a purpose."

Beginnings

Patrick arrived with the force of a tornado, not giving me time to adjust to the operating room or this thing called motherhood. First he was inside my belly and then he was out — screaming with will to live, and yet never quite mastering those synchronized first breaths. It seems it would be that way always through his life — conquering the dance of life one tiny step at a time, yet always a few steps out of sync. Always, it would be that way.

A few short months earlier, Larry and I reveled in the news of our pregnancy and celebrated our sixth wedding anniversary with a new focus and hope for the coming years. We were thrilled with our pregnancy but soon realized that people like to give lots of pregnancy advice, whether you want it or not. Rather, they like to tell you everything that could possibly go wrong either during your pregnancy, or when you start parenting. From doctors to teachers to other healthcare workers, to moms on the playground, everyone had an opinion and most were different from what we wanted or hoped for our child.

Advice on epidurals, formula, and breast feeding, which diapers to use and which schools to attend, were the topics of every conversation, each person insisting their advice was best. We were bombarded with information and instructions from magazines, doctors, teachers, and other mothers, about what our child should do and who he should be. It was difficult to know where to begin and what to decide.

Larry and I wanted our child to have choices and to excel in the world, but most of all to be happy and healthy — the same thing that every parent wants and wishes for. The reality is: that is what we ask for, but no parent is satisfied with just happy and healthy. It's a really good start, but if we are to be honest with ourselves, we want so much more for our children. Please let them not have the life struggles that I had, please let them fit in, please help them to be successful, to have friends and enough money to make it through each month. Happy and healthy — while not a lie, is just not enough.

It was hard to balance all the opinions with the experts and with our own thoughts on how children should be raised. Much of the advice made us feel unknowledgeable and incompetent. Many times my husband and I went along with advice for our child when it didn't feel right; when we knew with all of our heart and soul that this was not the path we wanted. We ignored those gut feelings, and pushed them aside because as new parents we were not confident enough to challenge what others had already experienced with what seemed great success. That little voice in our heads and in our community, told us to do what everyone else had done because it's a proven method or parenting style.

Patrick did not give us much chance to figure anything out when he arrived a full eight weeks earlier than his expected due date. Hard decisions had to be made — and those decisions didn't include diapers or formula, but whether we would ever be able to bring our child home with us. As this child has done with everything in life, he descended upon the world and ignored the rules that others set forth for him. This child challenged me and all I knew about parenting and education and family, in the most delightful and in the most heart-wrenching of ways. Patrick has taught me more lessons than I could ever teach him.

Trusting Your Gut

Wives tales tell us that tornados and lightning never strike the same place twice, but that's a lie. The first storm hit with Patrick's premature birth and then again a full month later, with no notice from the Neonatal Intensive Care Unit (NICU) that it was time for him to go home, and we were now responsible for him. Larry and I planned for over a month for Patrick's homecoming, but now the sheer panic of taking a child home with medical needs, scared us to death. First our baby was in the care of the NICU, and then he was leaving and suddenly ours alone to manage the next steps in parenting. And there was no instruction manual!

Our first pediatrician appointment was scheduled for a few days after Patrick was released from the hospital. The form that I had to fill out with all his medical history, asked a series of questions about whether I planned to have my child attend preschool. It seemed so silly to me that they would ask this about a child that was one month old, and whom I was just getting to know. I had already relinquished parenting and my child's medical care to others for his first month of life, and was not yet able or even ready to process the thought of deciding something for my newborn, that was years down the road. I left that question blank along with several others that asked about my parenting style. My goal for this first month was to occasionally shower if I was able, and to keep my kid alive. Parenting style? Survival!

The park became a frequent outing for me and Patrick. The fresh air and need for adult interaction became a necessity. But the moms on the playground were very convincing that if a child didn't go to preschool, he would be damaged and disadvantaged for life. These moms already had their kids enrolled in baby sign language and dance classes, and had their kids' college already planned out. To me, preschool seemed so regimented and academic for three-year-olds who were still so young and learning through play. Their days were planned right down to the minute, and there would be little time to do all of the things that Patrick and I enjoyed so much, like free art and going to the park. Preschool was the expected path to take, and playground talk from other moms was very persuasive that this should be the only path. I was still figuring out how to get sweet potato barf out of the beige carpeting, and how many meals a week I could make in my crockpot without my husband protesting another all-in-one meal. Did I really need to think about preschool now?

Throughout his toddler years, Patrick and I were used to carefree days of exploring museums and playgrounds or finding chestnut hulls in the fall. We spent our days cutting paper and building block castles, and learning about animals. In the evening, bath time lasted until the water was cold and we'd sing, *Splish-Splash I Was Taking a Bath,* until we both became silly and started changing the words. We spent countless hours baking cookies and rolling bread dough until it was so tough, it was inedible. Patrick was equally delighted to spend time with Larry, and squealed with delight when his car pulled in the driveway at the end of the day. They shared the bedtime ritual of stories and tucking in at the end of the day. It was precious time, that passed oh so quickly.

Out of the Box Learning

The parents in playgroup at the library were also hard to listen to. They touted how preschool prepared kids for kindergarten, and kindergarten prepared them for first grade. They talked about how no child would be ready for college if they weren't reading by first grade. The moms professed that preschoolers should know their colors and numbers, and learn how to sit in a circle and raise their hands. They said that preschoolers should know how to line up, stand in line absolutely still, and color inside the lines. It seemed so silly to me that someone believed they had to teach a child to do these things. Group circles are found in church, and at the library, and even when friends came over to play. People naturally form circles in life. Even cavemen had this figured out when sitting around the fire. Hand raising — well how hard was that? Standing in line was learned at the bank, deli counter, the grocery store and the zoo. Patrick already knew these things, and we didn't teach him any of them. He was already learning so much and absorbing every single thing around him. I joked with Larry, saying that's why toddlers' heads are so big — because they suck up all of life like a sponge that swells.

I was still so torn about preschool because the forced early learning didn't seem natural at all, and appeared counter to how I knew my child learned. Planning for his college before he learned to hold a sippy cup or wipe his own butt, seemed ridiculous. Planning for the future before the present even happened, didn't seem to honor my son or our time together. Preschool seemed so rushed and so outside of my child's inquisitive nature to learn.

Larry and I were not dissimilar from most parents in our thinking about the standard path in education. We were both the product of public schools and had done fairly well; and we assumed our child would follow the same path and also do well. Despite that inner voice telling me differently, we sent Patrick off to a local preschool that had a great reputation and was just a few months long in class time. Surely I could stick it out for twice a week for only three months, and if we, or he didn't like it, we didn't have to return. We started off slowly and only enrolled him in the two days a week, half-day class to see how things went.

Larry and I took Patrick to the preschool's open house and felt reassured at the classroom's welcoming feel. Dress-up corners, and wooden blocks, and space to create art — it was calming and lovely. He would start his day with circle time and recite the pledge of allegiance, do a weather chart and sing the morning song. There would be a snack and some outside playtime, and he would learn his letters and sounds, and how to write his name.

Patrick was very excited to start at his new school. We bought him a backpack but he had to leave his beloved stuffed rabbit, Bun-Bun, behind at home. On the first day, I stayed with Patrick for just a few minutes in the hall, before the teachers began to gather the children for morning circle. Standing next to us, a few kids were crying and didn't want their parents to leave. For many of them, my child included, this was their first formal experience away from Mom or Dad with complete strangers. It was heart-wrenching to watch and many of the parents were struggling as much, if not more than the kids. The moms at the playground told me this was a rite of passage and that all kids (and parents), go through this.

I met the director of the school a few weeks earlier during orientation, but she wasn't there to greet parents on the first day of preschool, and the head teacher was just hired the week before. No one had met her before the door opened and she busied herself with greeting parents, and shuffling kids through the doorway of the preschool. She met each child on her knees, then wrapped her arms around them, and smiled as widely as she possibly could. She and the teacher's assistant oohed and aaahed at the backpacks and pretty dresses, and light up sneakers, and quickly placed a name tag around each child's neck. There was little time for anything else but a brief hello and introduction for the parents. The staff handed papers to each of the parents that told us about pickup procedures for the end of class, and then the door closed.

Out of the Box Learning

Walking back out to my car, I wondered in what other life circumstance I would leave my child with a complete stranger, having never met them. When might I ever let someone close the door, disappear with my child, and tell me to come back in a few hours? I knew nothing about the teacher or helpers in the class either, and a sense of panic suddenly spread over me. But the other parents didn't seem to struggle with this, so I sheepishly turned away and walked back to my car.

During preschool time, I sat in my car in the parking lot for the entire two-and-a-half hours reading a book and watching the minutes tick ever so slowly by. I walked back to the classroom a full fifteen minutes before dismissal time. There were several other parents, all waiting anxiously for the door to open and for their child to be released. A sign on the classroom door said,

Please Do Not Knock or Enter Classroom.
Dismissal Time is 11:30 a.m.

At eleven-thirty, the teachers sent the students out one by one, cattle-branding style, through the door, to assure the right parent had the right child after we flashed our identification and they verified our name on the pickup list. There was no time to ask the teacher any questions and all fifteen kids were out the door in a matter of ten minutes. The teachers hurriedly disappeared back into the classroom so that they could prepare for the next class arriving, in half an hour.

Patrick adjusted to the preschool routine after about four classes. He didn't like leaving whatever he was doing at home to get in the car and go to school, but was content enough once he settled into the class. He would much rather do activities by himself, according to the notes that were put in his lunch box from the teacher. The colorful classroom notes said, *Today I played with____*. His end of the day notes always said he played in the sand table or did art, but there were never any playmates listed, or names of his classmates. He enjoyed circle time and the fish tank in the classroom too, but we saw little interaction with his classmates — at least on the notes.

At open house, one of the few times parents were allowed into the room, Patrick went off by himself to play with the sensory table. He proudly showed me everything in his classroom and guided me around the bright space. But when I asked him who his classmates were, he did not remember one child's name, and no children approached him to play or talk to him. I thought it was odd, but the day itself was overwhelming and other children were looking lost in the noise and chaos as well.

After a few months, the preschool sent a report card home on Patrick's progress. I didn't actually care if he knew his numbers or letters because he was three, but they marked him as progressing. I wanted to know about his heart and if he was making friends, but they told me he couldn't yet button or lace things; that he was only able to draw primitive looking people, and by now his people drawings should have more details like ears and hair and clothing. I saw the hearts drawn around his colorful family, the pictures of our dogs with wagging tails, and the rainbows over our yard in his drawings. They saw lack of skill and stick figures.

The preschool days marched on, but I sensed something was off with Patrick. He hit all of the developmental milestones a child of his age should, but there was something quirky and off-putting about his mannerisms. Larry noticed it too. I couldn't quite figure out what was different about this child, but there was an angst deep in my gut that something was not right. His well child appointments with the pediatrician were uneventful; though we expressed our concern about our son's development. The doctor kept telling us that for Patrick's adjusted age for his prematurity, he was doing just fine.

As the year progressed, we noticed more oddities with our son such as his heightened sensitivity to the plight of all living things. One day after a hot summer rain, I was leaving the house to buy groceries. Hundreds of worms descended upon our driveway trying to escape the heavy flooding of their now soaked holes in the ground. As I started to back out of the driveway, Patrick burst out the front door, screaming in absolute terror. "Don't back up, Mommy, please don't back up," he cried. "You'll kill the worms!" His state of panic and despair frightened me.

There was no calming him down as tears fell from his eyes in large drops, snot poured from his nose, and his chest heaved with grief in big hiccups. I could not console him, and it was only after convincing him that the worms would go back to their dirt lairs after dark and would not be killed in the driveway, that I could attempt my shopping again.

Patrick's cautious nature, quirky mannerisms and need for order had us deeply concerned. We had never heard of a three-year-old being able to, or even wanting to organize a Tupperware cabinet. He would have a complete meltdown when the matching lids were not placed with the right sized container, or if the shampoo bottles weren't exactly lined up in the shower with the labels facing outward. Used bars of soap that melted in the hot shower were unacceptable, and we switched to liquid soap when his bouts of running around the bathtub to avoid the squishy, used soap, exhausted us.

Clothing tags drove him to insanity and led to many episodes of nakedness. Shoes and socks were a particular problem and had to feel just right. They could not be the kind that laced up because they would start too tight and end up too loose, and they made his feet sweat. I didn't bother replacing lost socks because Patrick never wore them, and was barefoot all the time even in the cold winter. It made outdoor play in snowy weather, particularly challenging. Other mothers gave me the sideways, one-eyebrow raised look of, *"Well aren't you an inept parent — letting your kid outside in the cold weather without socks or shoes."* Any outing to where he should be wearing shoes and socks became a wrestling match, which Larry and I usually lost.

There were many things with Patrick that seemed out of sync compared to other children his age; like the time at eighteen months when he built a perfectly formed dinosaur out of wooden, colored blocks. It had a smallish, triangular, shaped head, larger curved body made from a half-round block and a long slender, triangular tail with tail plates or spikes along its back, made from even smaller triangular blocks. All of the scales matched in color, and the size of the scales decreased as you went further down the tail of his creation. There was no denying it was a dinosaur because Patrick found the pack of dinosaur flash cards and labeled his creation, "Stegosaurus."

Other children his age were stacking blocks and knocking them down, but Patrick could not cope with unorganized blocks, or much of anything in disarray. Stacking blocks provided little stimulation for this child, and knocking them down was devastating to him, and sent him into a panic to return them to order. If he wanted to build a new tower, he would carefully deconstruct the first, sort the blocks by shape or size and then assiduously build something new. Despite all of these things, Larry and I continued to be reassured by the doctors that everything was okay, and we ignored what our eyes and head were telling us; that something was just not right with our child.

As our son grew, Larry and I longed for another child. Patrick seemed past his medical issues and concerns from his premature birth, and life was settled and good. We thought two children would round out our family but after several more miscarriages and failed invitro attempts, we were heartbroken and tired of the roller coaster. When we decided to adopt, a newborn baby girl from South Korea was matched with us, just ten short months after we filed our initial paperwork. Our daughter, Morgan, came home to us just two weeks before Christmas at four months old. Two kids stretched us financially and emotionally, and for a while we put aside our concern about the quirkiness in our three-year-old and chalked it up to immaturity so that we could focus on our new family member. Morgan was a delightful baby—shock black hair with a faux hawk and cupid-kissed lips with pink porcelain skin. Patrick adored her and even on his sister's most crabby, colicky days, could manage to make her smile.

• • •

Out of the Box Learning

Larry and I were becoming very cramped in our little nine-hundred square foot house with two children and a menagerie of pets. While we were house hunting, my mother called to tell us that my father's cancer returned after six years in remission, and that he would need more chemo and radiation. Mom was struggling to keep up with all the medical appointments and caring for him. Larry and I decided to find a house with an in-law apartment so that my parents could move in and be closer, rather than an hour and a half away. The apartment would give my parents their own space, and allow me to help with dad's medical care more easily since I was still working at the hospital as an ICU nurse.

We found a house with an in-law apartment over the garage and the kids were delighted that their Granny and Grampy would be here with them. We were thrilled that our children were finally going to be able to get to know their grandparents and have a relationship with them on a more regular basis.

A few months after we settled into our new home, Mom and Dad joined us. It took weeks of getting the new doctors' appointments, but Mom seemed to relax knowing that I had access to the doctors at the hospital. She had grown weary of caring for Dad, and left a lot of it to me. Dad was healing remarkably well once again after more radiation, and the following summer we planted an enormous garden together in our backyard. He would get winded turning over the soil, but Larry and I and the kids helped, and soon enough we had enough produce to supply the whole neighborhood.

I cherished the time in the garden with Dad. We'd hoe a little, rest on the handle, and chat and then pull some weeds. He'd give me all the gardening tips he knew, and the neat rows of vegetables sitting in the freshly turned soil were like a work of art. I was reminded of gentler days of my childhood in the garden with him and how much I learned from his bits of wisdom. Patience at watching the seedlings grow, nourishing and fertilizing the soil for strong foundations, balancing the needs of the plant with what nature was already providing … so many things I learned and carried with me into my adult life.

    Dad and I met by the garden gate and shared our morning coffee. We talked while the cherry tomatoes listened and nodded in agreement about our gardening plans. My thoughts always carried me to Patrick in school and how he didn't seem to fit in. Even when he was fully participating, he just didn't seem to fit in. Dad rested his arms on the hoe and asked, "What is your heart telling you?" This was his way of saying he had no idea how to answer this question and so he reflected it back to me to figure out. I knew what my heart was telling me but my head would not agree, and I changed my mind at every turn.

    Nothing felt right about sending Patrick off to school every day when I was this uninvolved in his day. To be handed a weekly paper that told me what he did each day in a classroom left me asking more questions, and I wanted to share those experiences with him as I did from the day he was born. Patrick's weekly reports focused on his lack of academic ability, with little mention of his social and emotional concerns. His preschool teachers seemed unconcerned with Patrick's social development, and told us that it was an awkward age and social maturity took much time to develop. I wondered why they didn't think his academic work would take just as much as time to develop.

Butterflies

Public school still seemed like the thing we were supposed to do, so we sent Patrick off to kindergarten on the big yellow bus when he was just shy of his fifth birthday. I hoped that the teachers and professionals would help him discover his gifts and indeed, he did learn and grow in confidence and make some friends, at least during class time.

Larry and I continued to notice peculiar things about our son — things that couldn't be ignored as just developmental. He didn't interact much with other children aside from his sister, and although he enjoyed being with other kids, he much preferred his own company. The pediatrician finally agreed that we should have Patrick evaluated when, during his yearly checkup, our precocious boy ignored the brightly colored toys in the exam room; and instead took all of the tongue depressors out of the jar on the exam table and stacked them up for neatness. Then he told the doctor there were exactly thirty-three cotton balls in the jar that sat on the exam side table. Patrick wouldn't sit on the exam table during the appointment no matter how much the doctor tried to coax him, because the waxy paper that protected the patient against germs, irritated him. Instead, he would sit on the small chair next to the table and look suspiciously at the blood pressure cuff that hung on the wall.

Once the pediatrician made the referral to the neurodevelopmental center, I called and made the appointment, but was immediately overwhelmed by what the receptionist told me about this first appointment. The exam felt entirely too large and serious for a child of his age. Five years old was the earliest we were told Patrick could be evaluated because kids needed to be able to communicate effectively with their words during the long testing day. We did stress to the clinic that Patrick's vocabulary and communication skills were quite advanced and he was already reading. But the receptionist calculated out his birthday and gave us an appointment on the exact day Patrick turned five, as if some miracle in his communication skills would miraculously appear the moment his birthday rolled around. Yesterday, when he was four years and three-hundred and sixty-four days old he could not communicate. Today, when he's exactly one day older, he can. I filled out the four inches of paperwork that the office sent to me, and answered all kinds of questions about our son from academic skills, to hobbies, to his daily bowel patterns. "Really, they want to know his bathroom habits?" quipped my husband.

Dr. M, a stout woman in her late sixtie's with masculine styled hair, showed Patrick a series of flashcards; and his task was to name these everyday objects during this evaluation appointment. The very first card was a caterpillar and any answer of insect, caterpillar, or green bug would have been acceptable. He sat for a long time looking at the card before answering, and I sat waiting not so patiently for my child to respond. I silently prayed that he would get the answer right, and that the doctor would announce that our child was perfectly healthy and developing normally, and that we had nothing to worry about.

A few moments later, Patrick cocked his head slightly and told the doctor about the larvae, pupa and chrysalis stages that led up to the beautiful butterfly, and how you shouldn't ever help a butterfly or moth out of its cocoon. He explained that, in order to grow and survive, the butterfly must do this on its own — taking the time to stretch its wings and dry off, and stretch again, and take a breath. It was only then, after enduring the struggles of bursting forth from the cocoon, that the butterfly could fly away. "Butterflies never hatch on cloudy or rainy days either," he professed. They needed the sun to help them dry and direct them to the scent of the flowers that will nourish them and in turn, would be the nursery for future caterpillars.

Sitting in the child-size chair in the doctor's office, Patrick also identified what type of caterpillar was on the card, its native habitat and what color the butterfly would become. He pointed out the color variations in the caterpillar, but used words like chartreuse and eggplant to describe the color blending, that perhaps you or I would just call green and purple. And then he told the doctor that a caterpillar did not have any bones in its body. And when it moved, its guts moved first, followed by the rest of their body, so that it created a rippling effect as it climbed in search of food.

The doctor raised one eyebrow and peered over the top of her glasses. I heard a little chortle and throat-clearing escape from her mouth. She smiled and said, "Let's move on to something else." I sat quite smugly in the corner of the office, hiding stifled laughter behind the three-year-old parenting magazine that was covered with coffee stains and dirty fingerprints.

Several months passed, and Larry and I waited for the test results from this appointment to come in. I was both terrified and hopeful to have an answer to my son's unique nature; but at least with the results in hand, we could tell his school what was going on and the reasons for his odd behavior. Patrick became the topic of every conversation in our marriage, and while there were never any regrets of having this child, there were plenty of moments of wishing for normalcy and wanting to leave the difficult days behind.

Beverly Burgess

My heart ached for my son when they diagnosed Tourettes Syndrome and a seizure disorder, not because it scared me, but because I knew he would never fit into a programmed system of education outside the standard model — an educational system that would never grasp his unspoken brilliance and splendor, because it is a different shape from the expected.

As I lay awake that night and watched the moonbeams flicker shadows on the walls, I knew that this child was chosen especially for me, and I asked myself how I could ever be the parent he needed and deserved. How would I learn to face my own demons and give stigma and labels the middle finger? Patrick's soft heart and gentle ways occupied every breath I took. This child was given especially to me, first his mom and then a neuro nurse, to navigate the difficult waters for him until he could do it himself. It is the moment when you recognize God's hand in your life, and are both overwhelmed with gratitude for this child, and yet filled with loathing at the circumstances He trusted you with.

There were many prayers at night that began with, "Dear God —Thank you for trusting me, but I'm not really qualified for this job and I don't know what to do."

Unsettled

On the first day of first grade, Patrick's teacher took pictures of all the kids with party hats on for the "Welcome to First Grade" bulletin board. Every child had a smiling, happy face…everyone except my child. Eyes dark and hollow, his face red from crying and a party hat that he didn't want to wear; the photo stood out from the others in stark contrast. My heart sank and for the first time I realized how incredibly unhappy my child was.

As the year progressed, Patrick's teacher noticed his disruptions, odd vocal noises and inability to sit for any length of time at a desk. The teacher told us that the other children were having a hard time focusing on their work because of his noises, especially during quiet reading time. I imagined it was hard for the other students, but I also thought about how hard it was for Patrick to maintain any level of concentration or focus given his medical diagnosis. Larry and I wondered and asked what the school was doing to help *him* in the classroom.

Patrick's educational team told us that he was allowed to sit quietly by himself and read when his disruptions became too much for the classroom. I questioned how much instruction time he was missing and how that would be made up. How was he getting what he needed if he was constantly asked to leave the classroom and lesson? Just before Christmas, Patrick became sullen and withdrawn, not just in school but at home too. My parents started to comment how he was sad all the time, and Patrick told them that he hated school. He cried almost every day on the way to school and when he arrived home. It was such a sharp contrast to the happy-go-lucky child we used to know.

Patrick's first grade teachers were kind and understanding but noted he was "socially immature." Several months into the year, his teacher called me to say that Patrick was still having difficulty adjusting to first grade. The other kids had settled into the routine of the classroom and didn't cry, but Patrick was still stressed and seemed withdrawn from the class. Change did not come easy to him, and we asked the teacher for more time in letting him adjust.

As the months went on we didn't hear much from the teacher and figured that any issues were working themselves out, or were resolved by now, although Patrick remained sullen and still didn't like going to school. When we asked him why he didn't like school, he said, "I'm always behind the rest of the class. It takes me too long to catch up."

In early February, Patrick's teacher contacted us to schedule a meeting. He still had not adjusted to first grade, and the teacher was having a hard time managing his behavior and time in the classroom. He was unable to complete much of his work and the teacher and counselors asked us questions about our home life and how we parented. They inquired about his socialization; whether he was *allowed* to interact with other children at home and out in the world, or whether he might even be experiencing physical or emotional abuse or depression. They asked us which doctors we were seeing and what if anything, they recommended for treatment and medication.

During that same meeting, they suggested we try summer camp to get Patrick used to being with other kids. They referred us to free library story times so he could learn to sit in a circle like the other kids and work on his attentiveness. We were told to let him play with other kids because siblings couldn't provide the socialization he needed, and because Patrick needed to learn to interact with children his own age out in the *real world.* Larry and I were doing all of the things they recommended already, so we didn't quite understand the team's blank stares when we assured them, that indeed, our child was let out of the house into the real world to interact with live human beings. No, he wasn't abused. Yes, he was happy at home. Yes, we read to him and let him read to us and yes, he could stay on task. Yes, he went out in public and knew how to sit in a circle and stand in a line. Yes, his doctors were aware and we saw them regularly. Yes, he was happy at home. Larry and I felt very much cornered with their questioning, as if we had done something wrong, or that his diagnosis and learning issues were somehow our fault.

We shared the findings from the neuro center evaluation with the school. Patrick's educational team shook their heads in agreement. They asked us again what we planned to do about our son's behavior, and which medications the doctors recommended. Larry and I left the meeting with more questions and were as confused as ever. I felt an overwhelming guilt that my child was impeding the education of the other students and holding them back because of his own needs, but I also didn't see much of anything being done for Patrick to help him succeed in the classroom either.

During first grade, I volunteered in his classroom as the room mother and spent a few hours each week helping the teacher with whatever needed to be done. The time spent in the classroom gave me insight into the class structure, so I could see where Patrick was or wasn't struggling. Generally, his class was fun and inviting and everything first grade should be. Each Tuesday at one p.m., I would arrive and silently slip to the back of the class, where the teacher had the work laid out with instructions for the room mothers to follow. This day I was assigned to cutting out hamburger-shaped papers to be put together in a story journal booklet called, *How to Make a Hamburger*.

As I looked around the room, I could not find my son. I glanced at the teacher who was reading a story to the class, and she must have noticed my confusion. She nodded toward the back of the room, as if to signal his whereabouts but kept on reading to the class. I didn't see him in the in the back of the room, but thought that maybe he was on the floor by the bookshelf listening to the story by himself. I wandered to the far corner of the room, where I saw my son hidden in the darkest corner underneath the group table. He was bashing his head rhythmically on a chair seat, and I stood there staring at him, completely shocked and paralyzed and having no idea what to do.

The other students continued to listen to the story, but my son was lost in some abysmal secret world and no one bothered to notice. Left alone and in the dark, Patrick appeared dazed, and was having relentless bouts of vocal and motor tics. I stood there, looking over the tops of the children's heads and then back at my child, wondering what to do, or what the teacher was going to do, or what anyone was going to do. The fact that my child was under the table, and that it seemed perfectly normal to his classmates and teacher, left me completely bewildered.

I paced back and forth, wondering what to do while the teacher kept her eyes to the children and continued reading the story. This could not have been the first time this had happened; else the other kids would be far more upset, or even more curious about the situation than they appeared to be. The kids and teacher went about their business like this was a normal, everyday classroom occurrence. I stood in disbelief and despair watching my child trying to manage this crisis on his own. I kept looking over at the teacher — wondering when she was going to help me and help Patrick.

I finally sat down beside Patrick and after fifteen minutes, convinced him to come out from under the table. He laid on the carpet, curled in the fetal position and rocking at my feet, as I cut out the last stupid hamburger paper. My kid was in crisis, and I was still cutting out god damned hamburgers, not quite sure what to do with my child or what my role was in this episode. Do I take care of him, or does the teacher? Should I cut out the paper hamburgers while I wait? Should I leave him alone to work this out on his own? Am I the mom that should deal with this, or the parent that needs to step back and let the teacher handle it? I had no idea what to do — so I cut out hamburgers.

The kids finally packed up their belongings for the day, and I approached the teacher and said, "What's going on with that?"

"He doesn't like being with the other kids or following instructions," she said. "He gets overwhelmed and hides under the table, and we can't get him out."

I stared at her for a minute and blinked wildly, trying to figure out what to say next and have it be kind and understanding, but all that came out my mouth in the foulest tone was, "And no one thought that was a problem, or to maybe call and let his parents know? How long has this been going on?" I immediately regretted my accusatory tone, but at the same time there was something incredibly wrong with this situation. My child had been ignored and abandoned.

His teacher told me that the other kids didn't seem to have a problem with adjusting or doing what they were asked; that they settled in each day and could follow directions normally. *Normally*. And there it was — a direct hit to my heart! That word ripping my guts out in a way that only a parent could understand. My child didn't fit the mold. He didn't fit the expected, and was so unlike other children, that the teachers and kids chose to ignore him during an episode, instead of helping him. They chose to let a six-year-old handle a crisis on his own and left him, scared and isolated, to manage something he himself didn't even understand.

Yet, I also recognized that something was obviously very wrong here. In one regard, the teacher was right; kids don't normally hide under tables and bang their heads. They can usually listen to a story and participate in class, but my child could not. Yet, I knew that Patrick loved being with other children, that he could easily follow directions, and absorbed everything going on around him despite the fact that he looked disengaged. Patrick's behavior and the complete dismissal of it from the teacher and other students, left me so angry. That evening I told my husband what happened and he just kept staring at me asking, "But where the hell was the teacher?"

The next day I called the pediatrician and asked to bring Patrick in for a sick visit. As the doctor watched my tears fall in despair talking about the school situation, he thought we should have Patrick evaluated for learning disabilities through the school. The neuro specialist agreed as well. I had a difficult time understanding how someone with such high intelligence could possibly have a learning disability. Those things seemed incompatible with one another, but we wanted to help our son, so we agreed to the assessment. I called the school the next day to request an evaluation and was told that someone from the special education department would be in touch with me.

Three weeks went by and I didn't hear from the school. I called the office the next day and the secretary picked up the phone. "Yes, they have your information," she snipped. "Someone will be in touch with you."

"Yes, but it's been three weeks already and I haven't heard from anyone," I said.

"I'll leave them another message," she quipped.

Another week passed. Hearing nothing, I browsed the internet and looked up special education law in my state. I learned the school was supposed to respond to me within ten days, and it already had been more than a month since my initial phone call to them. I wrote a letter to the principal requesting a full evaluation as my pediatrician recommended. I noted in the letter that I had requested an evaluation over a month ago and by law, they had ten days to respond and I expected a return phone by the end of the day.

Out of the Box Learning

I requested an evaluation with occupational, speech and physical therapy, and the school psychologist, as the pediatrician recommended. In the letter I noted all the areas where Patrick was struggling, like poor time management, illegible writing, poor spelling and written expressive language, reversals of letters and numbers, and his social issues. I included medical information from his doctors so the school would have the full picture of what was going on. My letter was firm and filled with legalese and neuro nursing terminology, yet hopeful for collaboration in getting what Patrick needed.

In the morning, I hand delivered the letter directly to the principal, making sure the secretary knew it needed immediate attention. That afternoon the director of special education called me, sounding very official. But from her hesitation I could tell that she had to look at the letter several times to remember which child she was talking about — and she kept calling my son "little Ricky". She assured me that the district's lack of contact was merely an oversight, and that they were incredibly busy. She talked too much about why they hadn't been in touch, and said that staff was out sick, and there were budget cuts, and that they ran the special education department on shoestring staffing. She also assured me that Patrick would be evaluated within two-weeks, and I thanked her for her time and hung up.

Precisely at the two-week mark, Patrick's educational team completed the evaluation and I was glad that we'd finally be able to help our son. Surely they would see the same learning difficulties that I noticed. When I asked Patrick who in the school came in to work with him, he replied, "Just a reading teacher." He seemed oblivious to the evaluation and couldn't recall any of the testing that the school did.

Larry and I set up an appointment with the special education team to review the evaluation results for the following month. The entire team reviewed his test results earlier in the month, but Larry and I had not yet seen the document or any results. During the meeting we heard how bright Patrick was, how tender his heart was, and how he loved the pets in the classroom. Then they moved on to the evaluation results. They discussed his raw and overall scores, and pointed with sharpened pencils to the areas on the evaluation where he struggled. And then they emphasized the summary line that said, "No learning disability." They underlined another acronym that said, DNQFS. I asked what DNQFS meant, and the director smiled at me and said, "Does not qualify for services."

"Wait! What?" I yelled. "I don't understand," I stammered.

According to the director, Patrick scored in the "very superior range" in most areas, and was ineligible for any services at all. The team thanked us for coming and began packing up their papers to leave as Larry and I sat there, looking at one another with wide eyes.

Most of the team was already leaving the meeting. Larry and I were still sitting looking at paperwork, but also said that we needed some time to review the evaluation. We told them that we would like to schedule another meeting to further discuss the results because we were so confused. The director smiled and told us that since Patrick doesn't qualify for services, there really was no need to meet again. "Perhaps," I said. "But we're not clear on the testing scores or why he doesn't qualify for services, and I'd like the neuro doctor and his pediatrician to review this and have some input." There were a few seconds of silence and the team told us to call if we had any questions. Within minutes, everyone was gone; leaving Larry and me in the room alone.

First grade was coming to an end and I spent those final weeks researching what the scores on the evaluation meant. I poured over every internet site and special education book I could find, that would tell me about the testing results. I consulted with a special education teacher that I knew and asked her to look at the scores, and help Larry and I understand what it all meant. Despite scoring in the superior range, Patrick had some huge gaps and deficits in his learning and his evaluation results showed that.

One area where he scored especially low was in executive function (EF). From my nursing career I knew that EF's were central brain processes, that were most closely involved in giving organization and order to our actions and behavior. Kind of the engine of the car — if one piston isn't firing correctly, then none of the other systems can work optimally. In Patrick's case, his difficulties came with trying to initiate, complete, and turn in his homework and class work on time. He also could not pace, self-monitor, or shift between activities flexibly either. Add in his vocal and motor tics, and it created another whole layer of learning challenges.

I was glad that we had some answers but Patrick was beginning to feel like a big case study or science experiment. The focus always seemed to be on what he was lacking, instead of where his strengths and gifts were. As I continued to learn more about his testing, I couldn't find the occupational, speech or physical therapy evaluation that was supposed to be completed as part of his overall testing. The neuro-psychiatric evaluation was missing as well. I called the school asking if they could send those results to me because they were mistakenly left out of his evaluation packet, but they told me that those were specialized tests conducted only *after* a child is deemed eligible for services.

I was so angry by this point, and asked the special education director why the testing wasn't completed when there was a physician's order and recommendation for evaluation sent to the school. I questioned her how the district could make a determination for eligibility based on an incomplete evaluation. I didn't really get an adequate answer, but she told me I could appeal to the State Department of Education if I thought their evaluation was in error. "Thanks," I said. "I'll do just that."

I spent days searching the internet for information on special education and learned that the school could not determine Patrick ineligible for services based on his cumulative evaluation scores.

They had to consider testimony from experts, his teachers, his classroom performance, his doctor's advice, and evaluations in the specialized testing areas. They were supposed to consider the gaps in his learning and also include what areas he did well in. I dissected his scores and lined up more evaluations and another order from his pediatrician, his neuro-doctor and the neuro-psychologist, demanding that special education services be implemented immediately. The educational team reluctantly met with us again and told us our interpretation of the law and of Patrick, was incorrect. They gave us different information than what I researched and reiterated that Patrick DID NOT have a learning disability.

"How can a child with such severe executive dysfunction — be expected to manage, organize, memorize, and plan his days and assignments in a way that is conducive to learning, if you all don't even recognize he has this disorder even after it has been thoroughly documented by medical professionals? If you add in his seizure disorder and vocal and motor tics from his Tourette's — it's a miracle this kid can accomplish anything," I snipped. The team looked at us with blank stares and furrowed eyebrows.

"Um, what is your background?" the director questioned. "I'm not sure your personal evaluations of Patrick are helpful in the classroom. It's really hard for parents to be impartial. We have qualified personnel that interpret the test scores and make the determination of learning disability or not."

"Well, considering we are his parents and have provided you with a detailed listing of what we have observed, have given you his medical doctor's evaluations, his neuro-psych evaluation and, have documentation of the areas he struggles with on the testing that your department just completed, I think that makes us qualified. I've been a Neurosurgical ICU nurse for over fifteen years," I retorted. "I know how the brain works, and not just physiologically. At this very moment I am likely *the* most qualified person in this room to make the determination of what this child needs." My voice was getting louder and I had to sit back and breathe to compose myself.

Out of the Box Learning

Larry and I stood our ground and countered their every point with medical and educational terminology from the test scores that were in front of us, and still they wouldn't budge. We grew more frustrated. When the meeting was almost over and no progress was made, I had had enough and pulled the lawyer card.

"It seems we still disagree on several points. We'll have our lawyer take a look at this to determine if Patrick really is qualified for services, or if he is being denied unjustly." There was a long pause of silence in the room. The director pursed her lips and told me that having a lawyer evaluate the process really wasn't necessary, and that we raised some valid points in our discussion. They wanted every child to succeed, and she said the team would take another look at his file to see what they could do for our son.

"Great," I said. "Patrick would appreciate that. When can we expect a plan to be put in place?"

Enough

Larry and I found a Tourette's support group for parents and kids. It was good for Patrick to be with others who experienced the world as he did — a place where no one cared or really noticed his vocal or motor outbursts, because all the kids were doing the same thing. We wanted to help him, but also needed a place to share our struggles and worries with other parents who walked this path before us.

Patrick saw the neurobehaviorist regularly through the next year and had already tried a slew of medications to control his tics and improve his attention to task. His teachers insisted he was inattentive. We saw something different and often watched him work for hours on a project that interested him, paying close attention to the details. Even during his "under the desk episodes" at school, we were amazed that in the midst of a meltdown, he could remember the entire lesson that was taught, or retell an entire story that the teacher read. He was absorbing everything he heard even when it seemed he was in some faraway place. Attentiveness as a problem didn't ring true with us and in fact it was just the opposite; Patrick saw, felt, and heard every detail around him. Blocking out the extraneous information and noise seemed more of the issue than inattentiveness. His mind both intrigued and confused me as we figured out its inner tickings.

Once, while trying to complete a science homework assignment on different biomes, Patrick was to color the different parts of the landscapes in their appropriate colors. This simple task stumped him and when I asked what the difficulty was, he said, "There are so many colors I don't know what to do." I asked him what he meant and he told me that leaves weren't just green, they were many colors like yellow and some had streaks, and some were lighter if they were in bright light, and others were black in the darkness of the forest. He told me that leaves were darker near the veins and stem, and sometimes the top of the leaf was a very different color than the bottom. I told him that the teacher would likely be fine with plain old green throughout, but he insisted in trying to recreate the colors he knew to be true. What resulted was a messy mish-mash of coloring that looked like a toddler had finger painted, instead of the magnificent colors he described to me. "It never comes out the way I see it in my head," he said.

The medications that the doctors said would help Patrick stay on task and control his tics kept him awake at night, made him gain weight and contributed to horrifying nightmares when he tried to sleep. He had trouble telling the difference between reality and his dreams that seemed far too real and scary. He told us about the video-game-like images that played in his head, and the black curtain that obstructed his vision like a mourner's veil. He told us about his nightmares in the haunted house and said he felt partially blindfolded as he tried to navigate his way into the unknown dark and frightening recesses. The shadow people scared him and lurked in doorways, tormenting him with auditory and visual hallucinations. We didn't see much improvement at all, either academically or behaviorally when he was on the medications, and instead, had to deal with the side effects of the medications and lack of sleep. In many ways, things were very much worse when on the medications.

Beverly Burgess

There was one exceptionally bad week when Patrick went without sleep for four nights straight. He would doze off in fits and starts, had dark circles under his eyes and was both hyper and completely exhausted at the same time. We didn't sleep either and functioned on day-old coffee and cold showers to keep us going. In the midst of one of his relentless vocal and motor tics, I had to leave. I could not take one more second of watching my son trying to both fight and manage the symptoms of medication, illness and pure exhaustion. I was so tired and on edge and my patience worn too thin to parent. I wanted to shake him, or slap him, or just find the right medication to make all of this stop or go away, and in that exhausting, irrational moment; I wanted him to go away. I did not want to punish him for something he couldn't control but I just needed to breathe, to have a kid like everyone else for once, and to not be a parent of a child with so many difficulties for one damn small minute of time. So I left — unshowered, and in three-day old stinking clothes — I just left.

"I have to leave," I told my husband through swollen and bloodshot eyes. "I have to get out of here for a while — I can't do this anymore." I drove for hours that night, I'm not even sure to where. Back streets and heavily wooded dirt roads with no street lights — it all became a blur. Even the animal's eyes peering out from the darkness of the woods seemed to be judging me — staring at me as if to say, "Someone else would have handled it better. Someone else should be his mom, because real parents don't lose their shit and walk away from their kids."

The radio was silent in the car because the noise overloaded my brain, but then I could hear my own crying and the judging voices, so I blasted some heavy metal music to drown out the voices in my head. I thought that maybe if I kept driving and didn't go home, that Patrick would be better off without me. Larry was the far more patient parent and I obviously was not cut out for motherhood or parenting, and who nominated me for this job anyway and thought I could handle it? The damp air and hours of crying came as

Out of the Box Learning

a relief to me, yet I felt like a failure once again in parenting my child. "What parent needs or wants to leave their child?" I thought. Surely, there was something wrong with me.

In the early hours of the morning I drove home. My eyes and face were puffy and red. As I came into the house, I heard Larry reading a story to Patrick. I slipped into our bedroom without either one noticing, still not quite ready to deal with anything remotely connected to parenting, or having to console anyone but myself. Things seemed calm and aside from the early morning hours, there was no indication that anything had happened earlier in the evening. Our household once again had its perfect façade in place. Through the crack in the door, I could see my sweet son, snuggled against his father — both of them smiling and engrossed in a storybook. My husband looked so beautiful despite his three-day old scraggly beard, messed hair and rumpled clothing. He was nestled in next to Patrick and it reaffirmed every reason why I married this patient, giving man, knowing that it wasn't intended that I parent or go through this mess alone. This journey would take both of us, each and every day in every way, to get to the other side.

The nighttime outbursts became a frequent occurrence in our home. Nightmares, hallucinations and side effects from medication were worse than the diagnosis itself. Larry and I switched parenting duties when each of us couldn't bear another minute of his ticcing explosions or seizures, or whatever other side effect the medications threw our way. We came to know each other's breaking points by a glance, the other stepping in when it was all we could do. Parenting by grace became our survival method.

My parents, despite living fifty feet from us, had no idea what was going on, at least to the extent that it was happening. Dad was ill, managing his cancer and we didn't want to burden him or my mother with more stress. I thought back to my own childhood when I was left to handle so many life issues on my own. Whether it was a death in the family or my school work, my mother rarely talked about things that mattered, and most problems were left up to me to figure out. Mom went to the obligatory parent-teacher meetings and looked at our report cards, but beyond that, there was little interaction with the school, and rarely any help if I needed it.

###

I knew Patrick's frustration and humiliation well. While I didn't have a learning disability, I did know what it was like to fall behind in class and not know how to catch up. Beginning in fourth grade I struggled in math. The prior year in third grade was interrupted by my teacher becoming ill, and then leaving her teaching position altogether, followed by at least six substitutes for the rest of the year. None of my classmates did well that year as we struggled to adjust to each new person's teaching style — if there was any teaching that happened at all. Mostly the substitutes let us play or free read. We had a whole year with almost no instruction at all.

The substitutes never knew any of our names and just as we were settled with one teacher, a new one came along. By the end of the year, the kids in the class were unruly and tortured each new body that appeared and attempted to teach us. It became a game to see how long the new instructor would last, the students taking pride in assuring that all who entered our door, made a fast exit.

I was so far behind in math and one day, at the very start of the following year, my fourth grade teacher was covering multiplication. The students in my class were required to recite the problem. The teacher asked us to give the answer orally and called on us one by one, up and down the aisles. By the time she reached me, I was very lost, along with several other classmates who shared the disrupted third grade year with me. I tried at first to follow along and then busied myself in trying to solve the problems as best as I could, but the other students were moving way too fast. When the teacher called on me, I burst into tears. My embarrassment at not being able to follow along or solve the math problems, either written or orally, was profound. Most of the other students seemed to be able to keep up. As a result, that year was my first introduction to remedial math or "the slow group." They gave our group a fancy name, like the Robins; but everyone knew it was the slow group.

I told my mother what happened, hoping for some help and sympathy, but instead she said, "Just figure it out for God's sake." I was nine years old and wasn't sure how I was supposed to figure it out. That's why I asked for help in the first place. I wasn't even sure what "it" was. Where do you even begin when you are lost? When I went to the teacher the next day to ask for help, she yelled at me and said, "All the other kids in the class seem to understand the concept. Why can't you? You should go home and ask your parents for help. I don't have time to get you caught up. You are a whole year behind."

Just figure it out. Even when I asked for help from my parents and from the teacher, the expectation was that I should know how to do this work, without ever having been exposed to it before. It didn't matter that I didn't know how to do multiplication; the expectation was that I should know, and if I didn't, it was up to me to find a solution. When I didn't measure up and couldn't perform, it became my fault. Or it was my mother's fault, or maybe the school's fault. Someone would need to be blamed and in the meantime, I still couldn't multiply.

I thought about my own parenting as I watched Patrick struggle. There were many times that I asked my own kids to figure something out on their own, when they didn't have the tools or past exposure to manage such complexities. Epiphanies while childrearing come often and when you least expect them, and parenting holds a mirror to your shortcomings in the most striking of ways. Parenting is always an eye opening experience.

My teacher saw learning my multiplication facts as something that should already have been learned and then reinforced at home, yet my mother put the responsibility for my education squarely on the teacher. Neither approach solved the problem, and neither helped me. I was stuck in an expectation that I hadn't yet met, and likely wouldn't.

Parents and teachers needn't give their children the answers to everything, but rather the tools, confidence and practice time they need to get started on their way. If they haven't yet learned a concept and you expect them to complete the work, or figure it out without any help, it sets the child up for failure.

Fourth grade was a turning point in Patrick's education too.

Endings

As we started what became our child's last year in public school, Patrick's sullenness and sadness never did go away as we had hoped. In fact, it became much worse when he started to exhibit signs of depression. It hung over us like heavy fog clouds and, just as we thought the sky was clearing, a new fog would roll in. Now in fourth grade, every day and every year up to this point had been a struggle. Most days when he got off the bus, he was crying, or over-whelmed or ticcing so badly, that he'd need to go in his room for a few hours to decompress. I had a permanent knot in my stomach at the end of every school day, wondering what new problem or event he had endured while in school.

Patrick's new teacher was a slight woman with short, cropped, sandy colored hair and firmly pressed collars, with matching polished buttons on her tailored jacket. She stood very straight, and her military appearance carried over to her perfectly neat and tidy classroom and obedient students. The desks in her classroom were lined up in impeccably placed rows, and all of the books on the shelves were sorted by subject; each having their own label to tell the children in which category to return them back to the shelves.

Even the artwork on the walls was hung in matching frames, with perfectly aligned spaces between each child's creation.

This new teacher introduced herself at parent's night by telling us that she was responsible for our children and their learning. We were asked by a show of hands if we reviewed the list of classroom rules, and she went on to explain her expectations. She said that parents should review the classroom rules with our children, and that the work must be completed as outlined. Late homework would result in a zero and — unless you were sick and had a doctor's note — don't even bother to turn in late homework. Sports practices, vacations and visiting relatives were not valid excuses for missing homework either.

Mrs. P's need for strict order in her classroom made it difficult for parents to approach her, or to be involved in any of the classroom activities. There were no room mothers or helpers in her classroom, and celebrations of any kind were discouraged. According to Mrs. P., fourth grade was the year when birthdays were no longer recognized. Mrs. P went on to tell us that fourth grade was the "make or break" year — it was time for the kids to learn the responsibilities of middle school that was just two short years away.

Mrs. P's years of wisdom and institutional knowledge were not something to be shared with parents and students, but something to be accepted as right and true. At parent's night we were instructed not to teach our children anything at home, because we had no idea what we were doing, and would "mess up their learning." We were especially NOT to teach them long division, or any math at all because otherwise they would need to be retaught the right way to do that.

My eyebrows raised and my head twisted sideways toward my husband. He would not make eye contact with me, and instead just looked stoically straight ahead. If he even so much glanced in my direction that would be affirmation or "marriage code" for me to proceed. I have seen Larry cringe many a time when my left hand raises and I say, "Excuse me." Right-hand — I have a genuine question needing clarification on something you just said. Left-hand — I have a rebuttal. "Excuse me," doesn't actually mean excuse me, it means I have an alternate viewpoint. A viewpoint I'm probably going to be passionate and vocal about.

But, I didn't raise my hand that day because I was afraid to. Who was I to question a teacher in a public school classroom? She'd been teaching students with great success all these years, so there must be a reason for her methods. But my lip was twitching sitting in that chair as I thought about my own child and his learning needs.

Halfway through the semester at open house, I eagerly made my way into Patrick's classroom with the other parents. I was hopeful that his beautiful, creative work would be displayed on the walls with the other children's, and that his work would be marked with smiley faces or "Great Job."

Then I saw the *Wall of Shame*. It was really called the Wall of Fame, according to the bright blue lettering on the bulletin board, but that seemed to be only for the kids that did well. Fame and fortune and gold stars and green lights if you did well, and shame if you didn't. I stared at the Wall of Shame as the night went on while Mrs. P. talked about Lexile scores, differentiated instruction, rubrics and standards. I wondered how many other parents were thinking what I was — that my creative thinker and alternate learner was going to struggle in this environment, with its regimented rules and expectations of what learning should look like.

The students' work on the bulletin boards were exact duplicates of one another; they all had gold, silver or bronze colored stars on them according to how the children did on the assignment. The work was further divided in zones — green, yellow and red — like a traffic light. The students that completed all of their work, had the neatest handwriting, those who did the assignment exactly as prescribed and turned it in on time, were at the top of the green zone on the Wall of Fame. Gold stars for these hard working kids! It seemed more an exercise in compliance, rather than learning.

Beverly Burgess

    I looked for Patrick's name at the top of the chart or even in the middle, then noticed he was down at the very bottom in the "red zone" with two other students. I thought it must be a mistake. Another parent whose child was also in the red zone was yelling at his wife, asserting that their child should be doing better, and that he should be trying harder, and why couldn't he ever be like everyone else?

    A parent standing next to me whispered to her friend, "I'm glad that's not my kid in the red zone." My head turned fast to look at them and I'm sure they realized it was my child they were speaking about. They grabbed each other's shoulders and laughed and snorted like highschool girls, as they hurried on to the next wall display. My heart ached with so much pain for my child and tears began to well in my eyes. There had to be a better way for him, a better way for the different learners where their successes could be recognized like the other children's work. My head started swirling and the very fundamentals of what I had always believed about education and learning, began to unravel that night.

    It was visibly clear that anyone who could not keep up with the rest of the class or learn as all the other students did, would not succeed in this classroom. Fill in the dots, do it as instructed, don't veer from the task and don't ask for a different plan. Comply and conform. No alternate learning styles were allowed in this classroom! Except that is what my son needed and that is what every child needs and deserves. I was not ashamed of Patrick's work, but of this system that punished those that tried the hardest. I glanced around the room and wondered if the other parents knew that I was the mother of the child in the red zone. Were those parents thinking that I didn't care or didn't spend any time helping my son? Did they think his intelligence was lacking? Or maybe, they only noticed how well their own child was doing and as long as they were in the green zone, all was well. The red zone kids were somebody else's problem. I was grateful that Patrick was not here tonight to witness this defeat once again.

• • •

Out of the Box Learning

I was close to tears in that classroom and made a fast exit out of the building. Sitting in my car, I rested my forehead on the steering wheel and bawled. Slumped into the seat, I wondered how my son had endured such disappointment day after day, and more importantly, how we, as his parents didn't recognize how much he was struggling. How did we let it go on for so long?

My son, who worked harder than any child I knew to get through his school work, was in the dreaded red zone, and he had to look at that defeat every single day. Everyone else in the classroom saw his defeat too. Red zone kids didn't get recess and they had their snack time taken away, so that they could do even more work that they couldn't complete or understand the first time around. Red Zone kids got extra dittos to do, and were labeled the nonconformists, the underperformers and the troublemakers. They were the different kids, the outcasts, and the forgottens. They were the kids that needed the most help and got the least and were shamed into performing better, doing better, and being better. They were the kids that gave their best every day only to be told, it wasn't ever good enough.

"It inspires kids to work harder when they see how well their classmates are doing," said Mrs. P. Except it doesn't, because my child was already working as hard as he could and not getting anywhere. Patrick was being rewarded with more work, red zones and punishments. Like most special needs children, they try just as hard, if not harder, than those children for whom learning comes "naturally."

"How do I show Mrs. P. how hard Patrick is working?" I cried to Larry.

"You can't," he said. "His best work and best effort will never be enough. He will never meet their standard."

Beverly Burgess
###

There is a kind of grieving that exists for parents with a special needs child. The hopes and dreams I had for my son diminished a little more each day as I watched him struggle in his education. When he was first diagnosed, I had hope that he would outgrow his disabilities with age, that he would function as easily as other children do. You have to hope because it is what keeps you going; to be able to take another step, day after day, through the muck of parenting a special needs kid. Maintaining that hope is hard when your child goes against the tide.

Alongside the grief, there is guilt. Guilt, that as a parent, I did something to cause his disability. Guilt that I should have noticed the signs earlier and pushed the doctors more to evaluate him. Guilt that he wasn't getting what he needed to be successful in life. As parents, we hurt and hope and feel guilty, because no matter what we do, we can't take away our child's pain. To watch your child suffer and not be able to fix it, is heart-wrenching and sobering. It's that terrifying place of being held under water when you can't quite catch your breath — when you wonder if you will succumb to fluid filled lungs because you just can't fight anymore; or if you will figure out the next tiny inhale, and maybe bubble to the surface and breathe again. What are we to do with our grief; our hopes of what should have and might have been? Where do we put that grief, and what do we pull out to mop up all the emotions that become part of our daily routine and sting our deepest parts so bitterly?

Each day when Patrick returned home from school, he exploded in vocal and motor tics for hours at a time. Homework was a nightmare and never completed, not because he didn't want to, but because he couldn't. He held his tics in all day while at school, to the point of being in great discomfort and physical pain, in order to function and not draw attention to himself. Ticcing left his body physically, intellectually and emotionally drained. His work deteriorated rapidly when he was tired, which was all the time. If the seizures and medications weren't zapping his energy, the rapid ticcing movements strained and pained his muscles almost all hours of the day. He went to school in pain, came home in pain and lived with pain constantly — and that was just the physical side of it. Emotionally, he was drained from failing and from being different; from being asked to be something he could not.

By the end of fourth grade we had been dealing with the special education team for what seemed an eternity. We attended meetings almost once a month for three years straight, and each time saw little progress and no discernable goals in Patrick's individual education plan or IEP. We asked to have the amount of homework he received decreased since after school was the worst time for his ticcing explosions. The team told us that they couldn't reduce his homework since it wouldn't be fair to the other students. All the students would then ask for the same privilege.

One entire meeting with the team discussed timed testing. Patrick's IEP included accommodations that no timed testing would be given, but the teacher insisted that this — along with writing the dictation sentences — was part of the standardized testing evaluation and without it, he would fail and there would be no way to evaluate him. We discussed retesting Patrick when he failed a test, and when it was clear that he knew the material or when his tics, prevented him from performing his best on the testing. Again they told us that it wasn't fair to the other students. No one seemed concerned that it wasn't fair to Patrick.

We asked for Patrick to be able to leave the classroom when his vocal and motor tics became increasingly loud and he would disturb the class with his Woody Woodpecker laugh. The team professed that all the other students will ask to leave the classroom at every whim, and that Patrick needed to control his tics, and be able to participate in class. The team told us that they didn't want Patrick to become enabled by the modifications he needed and that as parents, we weren't making him "toe the line," or were perhaps too involved.

The teachers and special education team saw the modifications as enabling our child; whims, added privileges, and special treatment even; rather than accommodations for him to function in the classroom. They were asking him to control vocal and motor tics that his body had no control over. "Imagine trying to hold in a hiccup," I would say to his team. They would all nod their heads in agreement and then insist he not tic. "But this isn't a behavior," I implored. "Behavior implies he can control it and that's not possible for him," I said. "He doesn't need a behavior plan," I sighed.

I gave Patrick's educational team a four-hundred-page manual with educational practices and insights for children with Tourettes, but they refused to read it. They handed it back to me and said they already knew about Tourette's Syndrome. I offered to bring in neuro-psychiatric specialists free of charge to help them understand the disorder and how my son learned. They refused, stating they had dealt with plenty of other children "afflicted" with Tourette's. *Afflicted.* I hate that word. There was so much more to my child than what they only saw as an affliction. There was so much that he could do, but they only saw what he couldn't do, and what he should do.

Meeting after meeting proved unhelpful and I learned to ask for the meeting minutes when on numerous occasions, the team and Larry and I, seemed to have heard different things about Patrick's education plan. I disagreed with the IEP and ended up rewriting it with the help of my friend who was a special education teacher. The team was upset when I pointed out that there were no measurable goals or outcomes for Patrick, and that his education plan was not specific enough. I voiced concern that marking "progressing" on each area of his IEP didn't actually give anyone, any information on *how* he was improving, or even what the measurement for improvement was. They told me Patrick's IEP was far more comprehensive than any other child's in the district, and that he was receiving more services than even those with significant developmental delays. "I'm not concerned with what the other children are receiving or how he is doing in comparison to them. I'm concerned with what my child is receiving and how he will progress," I said. "Stop telling me what he can't do, and tell me how you are going to build on what he can do," I yelled.

Larry and I began to sit in the silence at team meetings, waiting for them to acknowledge our concerns and talking points. In the years prior, we would try to convince, cajole and coax the team into agreeing with us. When the subject would go off track, we'd bring them back to our question and say, "Before we move ahead or get too far off topic, we'd like to get back to the question we asked."

The special education team ultimately approved the revised IEP, when we didn't back down. They tried to offer us something called a 504 plan but we refused. The 504 only addressed Patrick's behavior in the class, and since we already knew that it wasn't a behavior issue that could be managed, we focused on the IEP instead. Larry and I both felt the team approved it just to quiet our protests and constant requests for meetings.

"We'll meet in six months," said the director. That will give us time to assess the interventions."

"We would like to meet in one month," I responded. "That will be eight occupational therapy meetings and twelve specialist meetings. Surely, they will have some insight on how it's going by that time and then we can make any adjustments on his plan," I said.

The director told me that IEPs weren't adjusted throughout the year, only at the end of the year when they have had a chance to fully evaluate the child. "So our son could possibly be a full year behind when you implement new interventions for next year, based on his work in the prior year? Why would you pass him on to fifth grade if he hasn't yet mastered fourth grade, and you won't be evaluating his progress until the end of the year? How do you evaluate the interventions if you wait a whole year? Wouldn't it make more sense to make changes while he's in the current grade, instead of when he's completed the year, and heading to the next grade where he would start behind the other students?" I said. "If we wait until next year, he'll be doing fourth grade work in fifth grade. How do you pass a child that can't do the work?" I asked. "That plan assumes that all the interventions you have in place will work in their entirety and he'll be at a fifth grade level. Why bother evaluating him at all if that is the assumption?" I snapped.

The team reluctantly agreed to accept the education plan but once the IEP was approved, there was nothing done to assure that any of the interventions were carried out, nor did they bother to inform me when changes were made to the plan, or to Patrick's schedule. I called the school once or twice a week asking why his therapy wasn't completed as it was supposed to be. Each time, I was told the therapist was ill or at another school that day, or there was a school assembly or schoolwide testing, or the schedule changed, or someone was late. Patrick told me that if he did have therapy or a specialist came in, it was often for ten to fifteen minutes only and they gave him things to complete at home, instead of during school. His therapies consisted of trying to finish the work he wasn't able to complete in the classroom so the teacher could grade it appropriately. There didn't seem to be much therapy or help at all, but rather just completing the prior day's work.

Larry and I knew how intelligent our son was, yet the red notes of "see me" from his teacher told a different story. Class work and homework papers were sent home for me to make the modifications on, instead of the team making them. I sent the papers back unaltered, with notes telling them that accommodations for the classroom were to be completed and carried out by the school, not the parent.

Patrick was still struggling in math, in fact he was several grades behind, so I taught him how to multiply at home using a method called lattice math. It worked great for him, but the team left notes on his homework saying this was not an acceptable method to complete his work. They said that all the students needed to learn the same method, and he couldn't do lattice math for the rest of his life out in the real world. If we used lattice math, the team said that they couldn't test him on the standards required of all students. They also noted that they couldn't possibly modify all his work to this method, and since it wasn't in his IEP, we were responsible for these modifications.

We used this method anyway on his homework papers since it was working so well. We sent the work back to school so Patrick's teacher could see that he understood the concepts that were given to him. Stacks of incomplete papers filled his backpack each week. The team wrote notes to me in red and then underlined the words when I refused to acknowledge the notes, or complete the modifications on his work that they insisted were our responsibility. I wrote back with a black marker and double underlined my words for emphasis.

The pissing contest grew tiresome.

Patrick had dysgraphia and watching him try to complete any writing was excruciatingly painful. Written work took him an exhausting amount of time and he hated this aspect of his occupational therapy. No amount of instruction on correct pencil grip or rewriting would help him complete the task at hand. The motor tics in his arm and hands further made writing an impossible task for him. It physically hurt him to write, and the large amounts of copy work given by the school frustrated him.

One of the accommodations for Patrick's writing was working on the classroom computer. While his handwriting was terribly indecipherable, somehow if you put him in front of a computer, he wrote like the wind and his brain could keep pace with his thoughts and typing. The district provided him with something called an Alpha Smart Board. It was not a computer but more of a word processor. The screen would only show one line of his work at a time, though. The idea was that it would block out other distractions in his writing and help Patrick focus on his immediate task of completing a sentence or thought, and then help him to be able to build onto that thought.

Beverly Burgess

The Alpha Smart was only allowed in school, so we were unable to use it for any homework completion. Larry and I soon noticed that this technology did not work for Patrick. He had poor short term memory recall and really needed to see what he was writing in its entirety, to finish any of his work. I wondered how anyone could work this way — writing one line at a time and without being able to look back to see the work completed. I imagined writing this book or a play with just one line showing at a time, and how incredibly frustrating that must be to keep thoughts straight or to revise work. The processor required him to constantly scroll back to see what he had written and then scroll forward to correct it all, one word and line at a time.

His written thought patterns were now a disaster, and worse than ever using this new technology. His stories and writing were more disjointed than before, and he wasn't able to print the work to review how it looked or flowed on paper. We notified the school about the difficulty with the Alpha Smart, and asked if Patrick could use the classroom computer instead, where he could visualize all of his work. While they initially agreed, it was a rare occasion that they would let him use the computer and instead, kept having him use the Alpha Smart during class time.

The team noted that Patrick was not proficient in his typing, so Larry purchased a software program called, *Disney Adventures in Typing with Timon and Pumbaa.* By the end of the software lessons, he could type faster than he wrote with a pencil, but the classroom teacher said that it took too much time to set up the computer, and that he took too long to complete his work.

This was true; written work on the computer took a very long time, but it cut his handwritten work time in half, which we considered excellent progress from where he had been. His teacher and education team still felt that this was too long for them to manage with twenty-five or so other kids in the class. Instead, Patrick had to rewrite the papers with a pencil, and the team marked his handwriting as illegible, and he continued to do poorly on written papers.

Out of the Box Learning

Patrick's education team told us that the computer was a crutch for him. Larry and I were fine with crutches. We used and found anything within our means to help our son, knowing crutches don't usually last long — a temporary measure to help him succeed. Our only goal was finding whatever this child needed, right here in this very moment, to help him move ahead.

Patrick had an eighth grade reading and comprehension level, but the teachers said I was mistaken since he couldn't produce written results to verify his knowledge. Verbally he could tell about any story, complete a complex character analysis, and would tell how the author could have made the story better. He remembered minute details from stories, but could never communicate those ideas effectively in school. Getting all of that information that was stuck in his brain, down his arm to the paper, or computer screen, was not something he could yet do in a pressured situation. The school refused to let him do verbal reports or testing, because there was no way to measure the outcome compared to the other students, and no way to document the method used. Larry and I watched Patrick's spirit deflate as paper after paper came home with red marks and notes of, "Please have parents sign," and "redo." We didn't sign those papers, or any others, and never made him redo any of the work either.

I worked with Patrick daily at home on his writing. He would tell me the story and I would write it down, or use the computer so that we could save and edit the work. Somedays, we were able to edit just one sentence. It was slow, laborious work, but we kept at it. He had so many creative writing thoughts in his head and was frustrated when he couldn't get them out. By the end of fourth grade he could write a whole paragraph. We let him explore literature he loved, not just the fourth grade books that were assigned to him. He chose, *A Tale of Two Cities* and *Huckleberry Finn,* and devoured anything about marine sciences.

Spelling words were studied and spelled orally at home for practice. He excelled at spelling and vocabulary, but always failed his written timed spelling tests. We asked for his spelling tests to be given orally. The school finally agreed but told us that he would have to stay in from recess, or stay after school to complete that work, because there was not enough time during the class to do this, and to work with the other students.

During this long year, I also noticed that Patrick likely had dyslexia, or some other visual processing disorder. When I asked him to draw what he saw when looking at math operational signs, he drew multiplication signs that looked like addition signs, equal signs that looked like dashes, and division signs that looked like dots and dashes. He couldn't do math because he couldn't interpret the operation sign, not because he didn't understand the concept.

We sent the report from his neuro-psych testing with his dyslexia and dyscalculia diagnosis along to the school. We asked for more accommodations and a teacher trained in the Orton-Gillingham method to work with him. The Orton-Gillingham method was recommended by his doctors so that Patrick could have direct one-to-one instruction. But the school let us know that there were no teachers trained in this method, and it was not in the budget to train someone in a specialized method that only one student would use. And since his visual processing disorder was very specific, they felt the Orton-Gillingham method wouldn't benefit him.

Larry and I wanted an immediate resolution to all of the learning difficulties we noticed with our son. We began looking for ways to alter the math operation signs, and other areas he was struggling in, in a way that was meaningful to him. A simple fix of highlighting the math signs a different color and consistently applying that to his work, helped him make great progress in a few short weeks, at least at home when I worked with him. We posted a chart on the wall that helped him remember visual clues like apples being added or subtracted. Addition signs were always highlighted aqua, subtraction signs silver and so forth. We did the same for various letters like b's, and d's, and p's, that always seemed to be reversed. B was always blue; d was dark green, and we tried to pick colors that corresponded to the first letter of the sign or word, for easier recall. It seemed quite babyish to Patrick, but in a few short weeks he too noticed a difference in not only his understanding of math, but of written spelling words as well. Since he was able to refer back the chart as often as he needed to, the colors became engrained in his mind through sheer repetition, and it helped him figure out word and sentence structure too. I spent hours asking him what he saw, what he thought, coaxing answers out of him, and modifying his work at home, in a way that would work for him while he was at school.

All of our story and literature books were marked up with highlighter pens, sideline writing, sticky notes and underlined words. He read them over and over again until the words flowed effortlessly. Larry worked on math with him in the evenings by teaching measuring and wood cutting, and taught him fractions through drill bits and wrench sizes. I reinforced fractions by having him measure cooking ingredients with me in the kitchen. We saw huge improvements in Patrick's stamina and perseverance in tackling his school work. He was now using the techniques he learned at home in his school work. The improvements and progress were coming so fast to him, like the floodgates had been opened, and he grew excited about learning again.

We wanted to share with the school, what we learned at home and what was really working for Patrick, but our calls and emails went unanswered. Eventually, I didn't even bother to follow up on them. Occupational therapy happened irregularly if at all, and his teacher stopped coming to team meetings all together. All of her reports for the meetings simply said, "making progress," with no other comments or explanations. The many meetings with special education services complicated my understanding of what my son needed. We would tell them what was working at home, yet we were often dismissed, as if we were mistaken about Patrick's progress. The team would tell us what wonderful news his progress was, but then tell us our efforts were not how the standards were evaluated, or not how they needed to teach him in school. They declared that all the kids needed to be doing the same work in the same way.

One of our very last meetings with the school department resulted in state mediation, when Patrick's education team failed to acknowledge our many complaints. The team was shocked and appalled that we called for a state mediator, and could not understand why after four years of "working together," that we choose this route. The mediation process was divisive, but the state did agree that the school had not fulfilled its IEP obligations. They asked for more time to allow the team to fulfil Patrick's IEP. Four years was seemingly not enough time. When we refused and noted that Patrick's interventions were in writing, and that there had been ample time to both implement the terms of the agreement, and to correct the missteps; they instead blamed our son for lack of progress and poor intelligence. They blamed us for being too involved in his education, for not having high enough expectations for our son, and for not letting the teachers do their jobs. They pointed out that we were granted more meetings and services than most other parents in the district, and that they had been cooperating with us despite our continuously asking for more accommodations. Larry and I pointed out, that while the terms of the IEP were agreed upon almost a year earlier, the school's obligation to meet those interventions had not been met. The mediator told us that it was unrealistic for the goals in Patrick's vast IEP to ever be met.

During the meeting, the mediator stated, "Perhaps you should leave your child's education to the people who know him best." My jaw fell open and Larry held my leg under the table to prevent me from rising and throttling the person sitting across from me. All five of his fingers dug deeply into my thigh. Marriage code for "please don't assault anyone today because we can't afford bail money." Larry was exceedingly calm, but I wanted to scream at them and spew four letter words.

My nostrils flared and I started to breathe heavily with wanting to say something, but instead I stared incredulously at the entire team, while tapping the bottom of my now empty water bottle on the table in disgust and anger. Several people sitting at the table hung their heads and bit their lips; some busied themselves with doodling or shuffling paperwork. The school officials sitting at the table stared at the papers in front of them so they didn't have to make eye contact with me or Larry. Not one person spoke up for my son's needs in that moment. Not one.

I glanced around the table again at each person for what seemed an eternity; a deafening silence hung in the room. I searched each of their faces for someone, anyone, who would speak up for my son, but the room was silent. My heart hurt so badly and my gut started to wretch.

"ARE YOU SERIOUS?" I yelled. "Really? Not one person here has anything to say at all?"

I could not look at my husband for fear of falling apart, and my thigh was now numb and tingling from his fingers digging into me.

After what seemed a long silence, the principal was the first to speak. "Mrs. B. — I just think that…".

"Don't. Just don't," I whispered through clenched jaw and shaky voice. "It's far too late for this now. I don't need condolences or coddling or any more criticisms. I need my kid to know that it's not just his parents who have his back. Patrick needs to know that there are others fighting just as hard as he is."

I'm not sure Larry knew what to do. He side-glanced at me and then carefully took the empty water bottle from my hands and stood it upright on the table, fearful I think, that it would become a projectile missile. The tapping had grown to loud banging. I choked back tears, and my stomach cramped and objected with pain.

The truth is, I didn't want anyone to speak. I wanted them to see my rage and disappointment, and to feel exactly what Larry and I and Patrick had felt for four long years. I wanted their hearts to hurt just as much as mine did for my child.

Beverly Burgess

The meetings were no longer about our son. They hadn't been for a long time, but it took this meeting, with no one advocating for my child, for me to realize this. I felt defeated as a parent. In one short moment, I was resolved to the fact that this environment would never help our son to be all he could be. "I think we're done here," I said. And then we left the meeting. No more words or hopeful protests. No more fighting for interventions, or collaboration for what was best for Patrick. There was just nothing left to do or to say.

It was all I could do to gather my six-inch binder of papers as I felt my eyes start to blur with tears, and my chest start to lurch. I could not swallow the large lump in my throat as we made our exit in swift silence. The walk from the hallway down to the parking lot was agonizingly long. I burst out the front doors of the school gasping for air and feeling like I was drowning. It was done. Any hope that my son would succeed in this environment was laid to rest that day. Walking back out to our car after the meeting, Larry and I were silent. We stood in the school parking lot and I leaned against the trunk of the car and started to hyperventilate and sob. I had chest pain.

I looked at Larry and tried to catch my breath and said, "I think I'm done with all of this."

He nodded and wrapped his arms around me. "Yeah," he said. "I know."

I spent the next week crying in despair, not knowing what we were going to do. Had we been the overzealous parents who didn't let the school do their job? Were we asking too much of them? Were we helicopter parents? Was there a better way to handle the situation? Did we expect too little of our son, or too much? Were we strong enough to handle the next step? What was the next step? Larry was mostly quiet during these long days and we talked on occasion but, always had more questions than answers. We both felt so beaten down and mistreated, but for the first time had a clear indication of what Patrick felt, and had to endure every single day in school. I sat in this brokenness, fully aware of his life in the margins

• • •

of public education — always a half step behind —always not good enough.

I sat one morning in exhaustion and reviewed Patrick's binder —the six-inch binder loaded with notes, letters, progress reports, IEP revisions and a whole lot of heartache. I wondered how we let it get this far, and how we failed our own child for so long.

Then I wondered how we were going save him.

A few weeks later, the daffodils were blooming outside the kitchen window. I drank my morning coffee and realized that what those school officials said, was absolutely right. Our child should be with people that knew him best. Except those people that knew him best were not the school officials, or the teachers, or therapists. My husband and I knew him. We knew every quirk and tic; his learning style and his love of reading. We knew his philosophical viewpoints and signs of tiring. We recognized moments when he was at his best, and those when the world was too much with him. Larry and I knew how he learned and saw real progress when we worked with our son. We knew him, from his first breath and his first word.

We knew him.

The school year was coming to an end and my face felt swollen and permanently red from crying. My friends grew tired of hearing about the misery, endless school meetings and our grief. My family told us to sue the school department, friends told us to give our child more medication so he could do what public school wanted him to do. We were told to move out of state, to try private school, to call the newspapers, and to have doctors come speak to school officials.

Others offered advice on new curriculum that helped their child, and told us to try schools for children with special needs. The advice kept coming and our heads felt full and muddled, and we began to question ourselves and our decisions. We were so weary with grief, and indecision and anger. It was there when we went to bed at night and still sitting there when we awoke in the morning.

Beverly Burgess

"What do we do?" I constantly asked my husband, but he stared at me with blank eyes not having any answers either. We continued to put our son on the bus and threw out all the papers he brought home without even looking at them. We ignored notes from the teacher saying Patrick hadn't completed or turned in homework. As soon as I saw any red marks on his papers peeking out from his backpack, I would pull them out and put them in the garbage. We didn't bother to attend a scheduled meeting with the school, and they didn't bother to call us to find out why we didn't show up.

Our child had become a fixture in the classroom and a pawn in his own education. By the time the school year came to an end, we had tried for too long, and too hard to get the educational accommodations our child needed. One afternoon I asked Patrick what bothered him the most about school. He said, "Imagine that you are working on a farm. The farmer tells you and all the other helpers that the bales of hay must be taken care of today. The farmer gives all the other helpers a pitchfork for their bales of hay. But he gives you a dinner fork to do the same job, and you must complete the work in the same way, in the same amount of time." I stood speechless in front of my son, recognizing how deeply abandoned he felt.

The final meeting with the special education team was scheduled, and the plan was to wrap up this year and plan for next year. I could not (would not) attend the meeting out of profound sadness, anger and likelihood of uncontrollable amounts of sobbing. I knew I could not hold it together to confront Patrick's team about the damage they had done to our son, to our family and to us as parents. We had been guilted, humiliated, doubted, questioned and deemed "those parents," by the very people who were supposed to advocate for and help our child. We held out hope for too long that they would help Patrick or support our parenting, or even his most basic needs.

Larry went alone to the very last special education meeting and I stayed home to pace, throw-up and cry some more. Patrick stayed home that day as well, and I lied to the school and said he wasn't feeling well. I needed my son with me that day if for nothing else, as a reminder of the immense joy that he brought to our family.

The school principal attended all of our meetings now because communications broke down months before, and my filing a request for mediation with the state was viewed as hostile tactics. During this last meeting, Larry read a critical, three-page letter with both of our thoughts and did not allow the team to interrupt or comment on how we were mistaken, as they so often had at previous meetings. Then he told them that we planned to homeschool our child. The special education director said she absolutely didn't recommend homeschooling, but Larry just ignored her and kept reading. She noted that we would never be able to meet his educational needs, and that the school was the best place to accomplish this.

When Larry finished, he pushed his chair back and said, "I hope you all seriously consider what you have heard here today, and that you don't ever let this happen to another child or family." There was no more room for discussion, and no one commented or tried to stop him from leaving.

Patrick finished out the last week of public school fairly uneventfully, and we went obligingly through the end of school routines like the testing and cleaning out of desks. The anticipation of the last day of school grew immensely. My chest began to feel less heavy and I stopped crying... mostly.

Decisions

A few weeks before our last meeting with Patrick's educational team, we notified the public school that we would be homeschooling. As the relationship with the public school deteriorated and our son continued to struggle, we knew we had to find an alternative learning path. Patrick was our priority and we refused to let him circle the drain anymore. But we quickly realized that the cost for private school was prohibitive for our budget. "Now what?" I asked my husband. We blinked blindly at each another for weeks over hot cups of coffee and picked-at donuts. There wasn't any way we could send him back to public school. We feared his heart and soul would not survive another year. I feared our marriage and family would not survive another minute, never mind another year.

Just before the last school meeting, a friend emailed and asked if we had considered homeschooling Patrick.

No, we hadn't.
No, we couldn't possibly.
No, we didn't want to.
No.

Homeschooling was for denim-jumper-wearing evangelicals, not for a mostly liberal, sort of Buddhist, somewhat religious, but mostly spiritual nature lover, who supported public education with her tax dollars. Homeschooling was for families with eight or more children, and lots of chores, and farm animals, and for people who lived on meager earnings. Homeschooling was for weirdos and well...

No, we hadn't.

No, we couldn't possibly.

No, we didn't want to.

No.

Maybe.

Terrified is not even a word that can adequately describe how I felt when it was suggested that we homeschool. How could I possibly educate my child and not ruin the rest of his life? How would I teach American History? I hated American History in public school. What about chemistry, and how would I teach subjects like physics that I never took or learned myself? Our kid would have no friends, no social life and well, what about prom and student council and yearbook pictures?

We couldn't possibly.

No.

Maybe.

The summer had just started but I felt completely out of control in my decisions; I had no idea how to even begin homeschooling. Patrick's teacher assignment for fifth grade had just arrived despite filing our letter of intent with the district stating we planned to homeschool. Maybe if he stayed in public school, next year's teacher would be great. Maybe he'd outgrow the need for special education. Maybe the special education team would be different. Maybe I won't cry. Maybe he won't cry.

Maybe.

My friend and I talked a few more times about homeschooling when she reminded me, that we were already homeschooling him. Larry and I had already found unconventional methods to his learning, that ensured he learned in a way that honored his spirit, heart and cognitive ability. Naming what we had been doing these past years helped a lot and I started exploring homeschooling more through internet searches. What I mean by exploring is that I spent every waking hour on the computer reading blogs, researching statistics, legalities, curriculum, lesson plans, setting up a classroom and had four notebooks full of information. Then I showed my husband how *we* were going to homeschool, and he rolled his eyes.

Each night when he came home from work I made sure to share my pages of homeschooling notes with him, whether he wanted to hear it or not. Marriage code for jump on board or get off the train — we're doing this thing and even if we have no idea how, we'll figure it out, just like we have with everything else. We figured out how to help Patrick these past years and he was already showing great progress. There. The decision was made and while we both decided this was for the best, I knew the brunt of our child's education would fall to me. Surely, I could manage homeschooling. Right?

I had my doubts, and my husband had even more.

Our daughter, spent the past year in first grade of public school and thankfully had no concerns. Middle child and middle of the road, Morgan was perfectly adequate, and doing perfectly well in public school. This child was happy-go-lucky, easy and unnoticed by everyone in public school. "She does well," said her teacher during our parent-teacher conference. "Nothing to report."

Part of me was entirely grateful that she was easy and that her teacher had nothing to say. I could not possibly parent two children with learning needs. The other part of me wanted them to say something, anything unique about our daughter. Do you know anything about my child except that she completes her work on time and is cooperative?

Morgan spent the past year, longer really, in her brother's shadow. Patrick's needs consumed us and Morgan was left with our leftover energy and parenting, if there was any at all to be found. It was difficult for us to spread our attention. And for those things that were going well, like her schoolwork, we had to let them be and sit in the small moments of grace of not trying to fix what wasn't broken.

Then Larry and I decided to pull our daughter out of public school at the same time as we withdrew Patrick. We were so discouraged and still felt so beaten down by how we were treated by the school administrators and special education team, that we decided that we didn't want anything more to do with the district. We wanted our kids home and needed desperately to rebuild our family connections and ties. All of us were struggling with family connections, and our family dynamic had become about dysfunction and lack, instead of abundance and joy.

At the annual town shindig, I ran into Morgan's former kindergarten teacher and timidly told her we would be homeschooling, when she inquired about next year's teacher.

Her face lit up and she said, "Wonderful — how great! I have tons of resources if you ever need anything." She smiled and said it really was the best thing for children and wished us well. I left that conversation elated and feeling like I could do this. So now we were homeschooling not one child, but two. I waited for my paperwork from the district and two weeks later received a letter back from them with the approval to homeschool. Great. Now I can homeschool, at least legally. Now what do I do? I wasn't a teacher and had no idea how to do this.

Not knowing where to begin our homeschooling journey, I made a call to a local Christian homeschooling group. It was the only group I could find and I connected with another homeschooler nearby. She was incredibly gracious and really helped to calm my fears. The kids and I attended a few field trips and outings with this group, but then found a different homeschooling group that better fit our family's needs.

We settled into the idea that our children would be home with us and that we were now wholly responsible for their education.

I spent the next few weeks looking at curriculum with the kids, poring over choices, and spent the summer months decorating our classroom space. Hoping to keep everything contained in one room, I decided my office would make a good spot since it was the only room in the house with any space at all. In retrospect, I don't recommend using your private office as homeschool space unless you no longer want a private office. If you value your private space, use a kitchen cupboard or other storage space for homeschool supplies if you can, and gather at the kitchen table rather than your work desk. You won't ever regret that decision.

My tiny 8 x 10 office housed me and the kids and two computers, and I made use of every single square inch of space. We bought a large work table and got rid of my small desk so that we could all sit together, and have room to move and spread out. Maps and globes, and grammar posters lined the walls and shelves. I bought extra workbooks just in case the text books were lacking, or we wanted more information. The craft drawers were stocked with colored paper and glue sticks; I shopped the back to school sales in search of notebooks and pencils, and purchased every school-like thing I could find.

My classroom at home was all set up and ready to go. I could do this! Mind you, I hadn't actually started homeschooling yet. I had all the stuff I *thought* we needed, yet had no idea what I was doing. There were so many questions, like how to plan our day, how to do lesson plans, and what extracurricular activities we should do.

I decided on a complete boxed curriculum for each child, with premade lesson plans and all the textbooks and workbooks I would need to teach. The complete curriculum supplied every text book for every subject, as well as the lesson plans and answer keys. I was grateful for this because as someone new to homeschooling, having premade lesson plans that told me what to teach and how to teach it, relieved a lot of my fears and stress about homeschooling.

The big boxed curriculum even came with a report card template which I tucked away until the end of the year. I wondered who to send a report card to, or if I even needed one, since in public school the district reports to the parent with a report card. But now I was responsible for grading. How exactly did that work?

Knowing that much of the homeschooling would be left to me, the boxed curriculum allowed me to show my husband how much work the kids completed each day, and how they were doing academically. Since he wasn't totally on board with homeschooling, I felt like I needed to show him our daily progress, and to assure him our kids were learning and keeping up with their peers in public school. I soon learned though, that the only thing I needed to keep up with was my own kids' progress. It didn't matter if it was slow or fast, and the comparisons to the kids in public school faded away rather quickly.

The Summer of Transition

That first summer without public school was a blessing to our family and a sense of relief filled us all. Weeks passed as we settled into a gentler routine of long park walks, swimming in the pool and reading books just for pleasure, rather than having them assigned. I devoured blogs and every book I could find on homeschooling, and shared my excitement with the kids. Patrick's smile started to return, his shoulders relaxed and his fists became unclenched for the first time in years. Why hadn't I ever noticed his clenched fists before? His vocal and motor tics lessened dramatically, almost to the point of disappearing. He began building with Legos again too — something he enjoyed at one time, but ignored in recent months to complete what he was told was "real" learning.

We raised baby chickens and picked vegetables from the garden. Patrick studied the Cicada bug exoskeletons stuck on the willow tree; he caught frogs in the pond and found Praying Mantis cocoons. He read the entire Harry Potter series that summer and spent much time in the workshop with his grandfather. His confidence started to return and he was carefree for the first time in a long time. We noticed a dramatic difference in everything he tackled and his whole demeanor seemed lighter. We saw his love of learning return. Life seemed so unburdened in these few short weeks and the son that my heart knew so well, emerged once again.

In the afternoons, I would lean with my coffee cup in hand and stare out the kitchen window at Patrick and my father in the garden. They talked about plants and soil, shared snacks of spring peas, and dug the fat garden worms out of the compost pile for our chickens. They built birdhouses with scrap wood and created lunch from the gifts that they picked from the garden.

Our new homeschool friends reminded me to take time to deschool over the summer. I had never heard the term before, but they explained that it was taking time to get the ways, schedules and the routines of public school out of our minds. They reminded me that homeschooling was not public school at home. They encouraged me to develop my own philosophy on education, and to set goals for my children that were centered on family and not academics — at least for the first year.

That entire first summer was spent deschooling. Even though I knew how far behind Patrick was academically, we left the schoolwork alone for several months, and instead, reveled in the glory of summer and reconnecting our family. Patrick had been so traumatized by the public system that he needed time to heal and regroup. We all needed that time to relax and not worry about testing, or performance, or schedules. We wanted to focus solely on our children's needs and love of learning in an organic, natural way.

This summer of transition for Patrick was joyful because life was far less complicated. Gone was the stress of school and school meetings. Gone was the stress of homework, failed tests, and having his work put on display for everyone to critique. Larry and I canceled many of his doctor appointments that were simply follow-ups to his academic performance. I started to relax too, and did not realize how stressed I was from the years of watching my child struggle.

That first summer without public school was such an incredible time of family bonding, that Larry and I began to talk about having a third child. We didn't plan to have more than two kids, but somehow life tells you that you aren't done. That same summer we completed the application for the adoption of our third child. The whirlwind of paperwork and social worker appointments, and parenting two kids, kept us busy. There was new life and promise in front of us in all that we were doing, and we felt so much relief in those warm summer days.

The summer sped by so quickly and for the first time we weren't overcome with Patrick's medical needs or needs at public school. This new freedom allowed us all to breathe, and we felt free.

When the summer ended, we finally told my parents of our plans to homeschool. They didn't disapprove, but didn't exactly throw confetti at our news either. They surmised that our children would be lacking in almost every area from academics to socializing, despite our reassurances that we could handle this. They would ask me questions several times a day about things such as what books they would use, and how the children would meet other kids. They expressed concern about the kids' IQ and socialization too. Even if I didn't know the answer, I would tell them I found some literature on that topic and was diligently reading to learn more and would get back to them. It seemed to quiet their concerns.

As September rolled around, we began our first official day of homeschooling right after Labor Day. It took us several weeks to figure out a pattern of learning and how our day would be set up. We didn't always get it right. There were times that I didn't prepare adequately for the science experiment, or assigned the kids the wrong workbook pages that didn't coincide with the chapter lesson, but those were minor things to learn from and to prepare better for next time.

While the weather was still warm, the kids and I did our lessons out on the back deck. My mother would lean out of her apartment door and ask, "What, no school today kids?" I would just politely respond with, "Oh, we're working on nature studies today and enjoying the warm weather. Math in the sunshine is far better than

Out of the Box Learning

the stuffy desk." My mother struggled so much with our homeschooling, because it was far outside what she knew and understood. She did try to understand and mostly respected our decision, especially after we told her what Patrick had gone through in the public school system. Still, she kept asking when the kids would be going back to real school. Eventually, I learned to answer her with, "We'll see what next year brings, right now homeschooling is working just fine."

My mother came down from the in-law apartment to visit frequently during our school time, and it was becoming a problem. When she visited, she distracted the kids with conversation away from their work, and tried to engage me in her errand and bill list. She rolled her eyes if I gave the kids oral spelling quizzes, and they got the answer wrong as if to say, "Homeschooling is a really bad idea." Patrick had already experienced enough criticism of his work, and I didn't want any of the kids getting discouraged on their attempts to learn. I especially didn't want my new role as teacher being undermined by my mother either. Being a mom to the kids was hard enough, and I needed to build up my own confidence in knowing I could teach the kids and not feel like a failure.

Mom liked seeing the kids and watching them learn, but I had to ask her not to visit while we were homeschooling. She was used to visiting me in the morning when the kids were in public school, but we had to change that so my time could be given to the kids. Instead, I spent a lot of time with her in the afternoon once our school day was complete.

Larry and I did manage to keep some boundaries with my parents surrounding homeschool and I involved my mother as much as possible, mostly during art time. She was great at getting more water for washing out brushes, and loved to help wash up dirty hands, or was happy to let the kids read a story to her. If I had to run an errand, she was willing to help with workbook pages or reading assignments. As the months passed, her questions of when the kids were going back to school gradually changed to, "What are the kids learning about today?" It became easier to engage her in the kid's work, but at times I felt like I had a third student!

The first few months of homeschooling in the fall were rough for me, though. Balancing it all was difficult and confusing, but the kids seemed happily ignorant of my faults and small missteps. For several months I was very overwhelmed and wondered how teachers do this for six hours a day. How would I get laundry done and dinner made, and keep the house clean, and still work part-time? How would I keep my sanity at home all day with two kids that were homeschooled, and parents whose health was declining? How would I do this when I had three kids instead of two?

Each day, I made sure that the kids completed every single assignment in the lesson plan right down to copy and busy work. Our day started at 8:00 a.m. and lasted until 2:30 p.m., so I felt good that I had covered the same amount of material if the kids were in public school. I even scheduled in minutes per subject and posted the schedule to the wall. Should I decide to re-enroll them in public school, hopefully they would transition back easily because of the work they covered. Keeping them at grade level was my goal, but I soon learned I was doing it all wrong. The strict scheduling and school like atmosphere drove us all to insanity. The lengthy time spent on assignments and restrictive curriculum were one of the reasons our family chose to homeschool; yet here we were replicating those things at home again.

The timed work and completing a lesson or topic based on calendar dates were the exact things I wanted to get away from by homeschooling my kids. There were so many things I wanted to do differently. My kids didn't learn the material in a set number of minutes, or when I thought the lesson should be finished. Moving to mastery of the subject material as one of our goals, really helped ease our day.

But despite our new-found energy in homeschooling, the end of fall brought sad new when my dad's cancer returned. He deteriorated quickly and by late winter, he was bedridden. A rushed visit to his oncologist when he became weak and confused, led to a prognosis of only two to three months for him to live. Tim, the oncologist who I had come to know through my years working at the hospital, pulled me aside and said three months was a generous estimate. He said we should look into hospice care and that he would make my father as comfortable as he possibly could in the next few weeks. Weeks or months, my father's time was going to be short. Even as a nurse, I had difficulty processing this diagnosis and short amount of time left with him.

Deep down I think Dad knew he didn't have long. He was so tired and as he sat in the oncologist's office; I noticed for the first time how gray his skin was and how frail he looked. I thought back to his talk in the vegetable garden when I was ten.

"Just like the world, when those tomatoes get top heavy, you need some strong roots to hold them up," he said. I knew dad's time was short, but I was so grateful for the past years he was able to spend with us and our children, setting those deep family roots. My father was instrumental in Patrick's healing from public school. He saw our child for what he was, a fully exuberant, joyful and smart child who had an enormous heart. In his later years, after Dad had overcome his alcoholism, he seemed to have a way to look past people's faults. He learned to forgive even himself for his past mistakes and did the same with others. Perhaps that was our lesson to learn before he died.

Dad told the doctor that he didn't want further treatment, knowing it would not help. He just wanted to go home and be with family. I rubbed his hand softly and watched my mother cry quietly in the corner of the room. She didn't absorb much of what the doctor said, other than it was really bad news, and later that evening I had to tell her again what the outcome would be for my father. Larry and I had to tell the kids too. Our daughter was only seven so she didn't comprehend the situation, but understood that Grampy was sick and needed lots of loving. We didn't hide anything from the kids and wanted them to be prepared when Grampy was no longer with us. He was such a big part of their life that we wanted to make sure that they were a part of saying goodbye to him too.

• • •

Patrick, although he knew his grandfather was dying, still went about their daily rituals as much as he could. He'd run up to the apartment to say good morning while still in his pajamas, give the music box a few winds, jump on dad's lap for a hug, and then fly back out the door. He would read my father stories when Dad was too ill or weak to get out of bed. He'd make snowballs for him, and store them in the freezer for another day's snowball fight that we knew would never come. Patrick asked a lot of questions about what it was like to die and he wanted details. It was hard to answer him knowing we'd soon be saying goodbye to the man I had only come to really know in recent years.

Still, despite the sadness of losing my father there was much to be hopeful about. Our adoption agency called and told us that a baby boy in South Korea was matched with us. Though we were ecstatic, Dad's health wore heavily on our hearts. We were celebrating both life and death in the same breath—the holding on to new life, and the letting go of Dad.

Two short weeks later Dad died. Morgan did not understand why Grampy was no longer here. When she visited my mom in the apartment, she would look for him and ask where he was. Patrick had a difficult time with my father's death and missed him terribly, and we were okay with his decision to not go to the funeral. He asked if we could bury Dad in the garden and the thought made me smile. "We should bury him with a fish head," he said. "Grampy said anything you put in the ground should have a fish head "cause it will make new things grow." As tears streamed down my face, I knew my father was smiling.

I gave the eulogy at my father's funeral. The words flowed easily onto the paper and what I talked about was not his years of alcoholism and then overcoming that addiction, but of his education and love of family. Dad valued education, perhaps because his own was so lacking, and despite only completing elementary school, his heart knew so much. I never thought of my dad as not being educated because he knew more about motors and woodworking, and gardening and home repairs, than any man I knew. What he did learn, he taught himself. I was so filled with joy that my own kids were now part of the wisdom and education that my father built from love. What he taught me wasn't anything that I could ever teach them from a book.

Our house seemed empty without my father, and my mother was lost. That next springtime my gardens didn't get the attention they needed, and even the flowers appeared droopy and morose. But the spring plantings gave me time to talk to Dad and provided a bit of solace as I dug deep into the earth and began to grow new things. Praying in the dirt, I remembered his words, "You have to let go of some things so that there is room for new things to grow." So much had changed in the past year. We let go of public education, dove into homeschooling, adopted our son, lost my dad, and now had my mother to care for along with our kids. It was a lot.

Mom's health deteriorated rapidly after dad died and she spent a lot of time in hospitals and rehabilitation centers trying to regain her strength. She spent thirty-two years with my father, but just seemed to give up on everything after he died. The body cannot fight when the spirit gives up.

The daily trips to medical appointments along with trying to care for my kids was exhausting. Mom came home with hospice care too, when the doctors told us there was nothing more they could do. Surrounded by family, she passed much more easily than my father, and just a short eighteen months after Dad died. I'm not sure how I made it through that year.

I tried to continue with homeschooling while dealing with my own grief, but it was hard if not impossible. The mental and physical exhaustion was debilitating. In the weeks that followed, Larry was at work most of the day, leaving me with the two older kids and an eighteen-month-old to care for, as well as homeschooling. There was so much I had learned about homeschooling, but my mother's death caused me to second-guess everything I was doing, including homeschooling despite the fact that we had been at it for close to a year. The reality was I hadn't yet mourned for my father, and my mother's death added to my grief. Everything came crashing down at once. The tasks of death like funerals and family, and caring for my mother and her illness, then a new baby, caring for two other children — one with special needs, encompassed every day and every waking thought — and I was unraveling in the midst of it.

There was one day in particular when the baby was fussy, my middle child was sick, and my oldest needed lots of help with school work. The kitchen sink was leaking and our dishwasher broke; bills were piling up because I was on a leave of absence from my nursing job to care for sick parents, and our new baby demanded all of my attention. I sent the kids outside to play for a bit and stood in the middle of my living room and sobbed. I cried huge amounts of tears, my chest heaved and I screamed at the world, begging for some relief and help, wondering how much one person was supposed to take.

It was such a difficult time that I wondered if I was going to be able to continue to homeschool. My husband reminded me that life comes at you in waves and to not make any decisions when in the middle of a crisis. I didn't make any decisions about much of anything during those hard days and instead just tried to welcome each day that came upon my doorstep. I realized, despite my family's and Larry's support, that I had been carrying a lot of the burden of caring for others by myself, not just in homeschooling but in taking care of sick parents and new children. My grief really didn't have anything to do with homeschooling, but that is what I blamed, or rather what I thought I had to let go of to survive these difficult days.

There were days when life sat so heavy on my chest that I wondered if I would ever be able to crawl out from under it. There were days that formal learning didn't happen either, and instead I would pack the kids up and go to the zoo or to the park, grateful for fresh air and the breeze blowing through the trees. It was a distraction that kept me from crying all the time, and still I felt like the kids were learning something while we were out exploring the world. We took it day by day, sometimes hour by hour. And it was okay.

Homeschool Groups & Family Ties

Soon after my parents died, the kids started to miss their public school friends (or just friends). We were so involved in dealing with family issues, that we had not yet begun to make any connections with other homeschoolers. We kept our search going for a core group of friends in the state, because I felt I still needed support and still had tons of questions and, I really needed to talk to other adults.

There was one well-established homeschool group with a large following but it was loosely organized and mostly online through an email group. I invited several families to my home and we started gathering weekly for parent support, and for the kids to play and connect. We were lucky in that we had the empty in-law apartment for our homeschool group gatherings. There was enough space for crafts, play, and for the teens to hang out each Friday. Our large yard provided ample space for exploring and for the kids to connect. We started with ten families and soon there were fifteen and then twenty-five. Before long, we outgrew my house and yard and our new homeschool group was born. Somehow, I was leading the group with a few other dedicated parents.

Some of the original members who started meeting at my house remained members of the new, larger group while others moved on. The group was incredibly important to the well-being of my own homeschooling. The kids were able to make connections with other homeschoolers, and playground dates became a regular occurrence. Finding a homeschool group was just the thing I needed for my own sanity, and to help me and my kids out of our grief.

One thing that changed drastically and for the better when we started homeschooling was our relationship with our children. We talked more, ate more meals together, shared more from our daily lives, and generally it changed our whole family dynamic for the better. The kids learned how to be with one another for extended periods of time, and learned when not to be with one another (see the chapter on self-care).

While homeschoolers are together a lot, togetherness and individual space are both needed to make strong family roots if you are to survive homeschooling. Our family roots run deep and wide now; it's a huge piece of what seems to be missing from a lot of families these days, as children spend more time in longer school days, and more time away from family-centric life. Family time and connections are one of the most amazing gifts that I will always cherish from our homeschooling journey, and one that I continually praise when I talk to others about homeschooling. It is really what the journey is about.

Special Needs

The relief of being done with public school slowly trickled out of us, like a leaf floating down a lazy brook. Spits and sputters of the time spent in public school would occasionally rise to the surface, but mostly we were finding our flow into more tender days.

As our homeschooling days moved on, Patrick's labels of special needs he obtained during his school years became less important, and I wondered why we label kids at all. We all learn so differently, and the need for public school to correct what they saw as flaws, seemed wrong, not only for those labeled as special needs, but for every child. I didn't want Patrick to have the label of being special needs because it focused so much on what he couldn't do. I didn't even really believe that he or any child was special needs but rather, denied the tools and patience they needed to succeed. It seemed public school taught to the limitations of the diagnosis, rather than to the strengths of the child. Patrick and the other children labeled as special needs, struggled with the expectations of conformity and standardization put upon them. These were goals set by the system that most children would never meet. My son's brain worked differently, so all expectations for success had to be put aside until I learned how he learned.

Many of my homeschooling days were spent just watching him to see where he was making connections, and where he got stuck. With the labels put aside, I realized both my kids were exactly the same: each of them an individual with different learning paces and methods in putting the big picture thinking together. Nothing beyond that mattered. It didn't matter how fast or slow they learned, or if math was learned by the lattice method or by bouncing on a ball. We would do whatever needed to be done, whether it was conventional or not. If it contributed to their growth and learning, we were perfectly fine giving it a try. We started where each child was and then moved on, inch by inch, to get to where they needed to be. We embraced every single success, and built upon that. I saw the difference simple modifications could make in any child's learning and was thrilled with both kids' progress in such a short time.

I read every book I could find on alternate and different learners, and found that homeschooling was a perfect fit for kids who didn't succeed in public school. Patrick's inability to sit still and his vocal noises that were problems in public school, weren't issues that needed correcting at home. His label of learning-disabled in the public school system assured he would never be able to keep up with the rate at which information was taught, or in the same manner as his classmates. The goal of his special education teachers and his IEP, was to assure that he performed at the same level as his peers, and that he would be able to complete the standardized testing so as not to jeopardize the school's overall scores. The goals did nothing to build upon the skills he already possessed.

During his public school days, we consistently heard from his education team that, "We need to bring him up to grade level." Grade level was the mechanism of measurement in his and the other student's learning. It compared them to other students, not to their own improvement. The expectation for Patrick was that he would perform at grade level, regardless of physical or cognitive differences, and not according to what his abilities were.

When I realized that by homeschooling my children, they did not actually have to keep up with their peers in public school or be assigned to a grade level, it opened a whole new world for us. Homeschooling was the absolute best way to teach our kids that was both productive and conducive to their individual needs.

All of the therapies that were written in my son's IEP, were interventions to ensure he perform as the other students were in the classroom; not to get him to a level of understanding or mastery of his work. Interventions like, "Patrick will complete the math assignments," did little to teach him anything, only that assignments had to be finished in a certain amount of time. Neither did it speak to mastering the skill. It wasn't an intervention but, rather an outcome.

Behaviorally, Patrick would never, ever perform as his classmates did because he had no control over his vocal and motor tics. I thought back to things like the occupational therapist teaching him how to hold a pencil. Patrick knew how to hold a pencil but when your motor tics and muscle spasms prevent you from doing that correctly, why bother? Physiological misfirings that cause your arm to jerk, cannot be trained out of a person.

At home, we didn't work on holding a pencil correctly but instead thought, "What does this child need to write effectively and understand his work at this very moment?" What he needed was a computer and encouragement that he could actually develop a story, instead of being tagged a failure and told he can't write. Or worse, that what he was able to produce was not good enough. His time in public school with the occupational therapist would have been much better spent learning a typing program, so that he could produce work we knew he was capable of. The team might have looked into voice recognition software that would type for him, but instead, the expectation was that he would do exactly what other children were doing, in the same way, at the same time.

The occupational therapist told us, "He has to be able to sit at a desk to learn."

"You don't need to sit anywhere to learn — learning doesn't just happen when you sit at a desk," I said.

"It does in a classroom," she countered.

Patrick's occupational therapy focused on acquiring neat handwriting, and finishing dittos filled with copy work so his writing would become legible. What it should have included was keyboarding and computer use, because no amount of therapy would have fixed his ticcing that prevented proper pencil grip and legible writing. Larry and I wondered how much progress Patrick might have made, were he given the tools he needed to succeed, rather than trying to get him to perform as the school thought he should.

Our family asked us why we didn't continue to fight the school to get Patrick the services he needed because, after all, we pay taxes and are entitled to a free and appropriate education. They told us we were abandoning the public school system, and it was our duty to ensure that all children had an appropriate education. But an appropriate education looks different for different children. Continuing with public school and letting my child fail, was no longer an option. We tried for four long years to make a difference and in the meantime, our child was suffering. After all the meetings and doctor visits, another year passed, while we still received inadequate services for our child with little progress to show. Each year, we had to begin the battle again and then our child was even further behind. How long do we wait and hope for results just because the education is free or the expected path?

When we first removed Patrick from public school, the special education department contacted us by mail with a very official looking package. They were inquiring if we wanted to continue special education services even though we were homeschooling. By law, we were entitled to those services. I sent the letter back to the district and cc'd all the subspecialties like occupational therapy. On the bottom of the letter we wrote, "We are discontinuing all special education services from this district." And with that, we were done. One week later I received the dissolution of services papers. There was no note other than to "sign here," which I obligingly did for the first time in four long years. I added a smiley face to the end of my signature for emphasis.

Still, we grieved having lost public education as an option for our kids. Homeschooling still seemed outside the norm, and we wanted our kids to have every opportunity that was available to them. While public school didn't in any way provide those opportunities, we still weren't sure that homeschooling would either. The choices to live out this new journey, and to learn how to begin a new story for our family; would come in the wake of grief, as we moved on toward something new.

For many months, I sat in my own righteousness at my child being wronged. It is harder to be understanding, than to posture though. Where the school district and I could not meet was on basic philosophical differences of what learning looked like. Their goal was to make him perform like his peers, mine was to allow him to be who he needed to be, in whatever way I could get him there.

Patrick was improving by leaps and bounds at home. We gained confidence in what we were trying with him, and rejoiced because our son was excelling in all he tried. Ending Patrick's IEP and special education services turned out to be the best choice we made for him. I wished, at the most basic level, I had realized that bit of wisdom earlier in my child's education.

At home, Patrick's difficulty with staying on task, fidgeting, outbursts, and sensory overload seem to dissipate almost immediately. His vocal and motor tics all but disappeared within six months of being home. The neuro-psychology center was stunned at the difference in Patrick's calm demeanor at his next appointment, and gladly started him on a tapered dose of his medications until finally, they were stopped completely. Once off the medications, his nightmares stopped too. We knew that he would still have vocal and motor tics, but the stress of not being in public school helped these to subside greatly too. The vocalizations and jerky movements became a part of everyday life, not something to be fixed or managed.

When Patrick left fourth grade, he could only complete three math problems. Not three pages, just three problems. His writing resembled that of a kindergartener. Yet at each IEP meeting, Larry and I were told he was making progress. I was incredibly angry at how far behind he really was, and how he was passed along from grade to grade with no measurable progress at all.

Each day that I worked with him revealed new gaps in his learning. I discovered he had no concept of punctuation in writing. He didn't know why or when you use a question mark, or a period, or when to start a new paragraph. I had extensive lists of things we needed to work on and one by one, we made our way down the list. We spent time on the basic skills he seemed to be missing instead of lessons from books. In a sense — that whole first year of home-schooling was relearning foundational skills. I set to work on mastery of the concepts, rather than completion of a full paper or page of problems. I got rid of anything that added stress like timed testing or vast amounts of writing.

The amount of work completed wasn't important at this early stage, the understanding and mastery was. If he could only get through four math problems that day, then tomorrow we'd try for five. If he regressed and could only do three problems, we'd try again another time. I broke every single learning experience down into microcosms, noting the exact point he got stuck. Not understanding what was just taught? Great— let's back up and find the very last thing you did understand, and start again. His learning became a dance.

I worked on his gross and fine motor skills with lots of time at the playground, free drawing with chalk on sidewalks, and art without guidelines. I didn't grade any of his papers and focused on process rather than outcome. My only requirement was that he try his best and try again if needed. Patrick's dysgraphia and illegible handwriting, never did really improve. I let him use the computer where his creative writing could become a reality, instead of disjointed thoughts floating in his head. As his writing on the computer improved, his handwriting began to improve as well. I have no explanation for it, other than there was no stress of producing writing that was a certain length, or just wasn't important to him. Once the pressure to perform was removed, he improved in almost all other areas.

I reduced the amount of work required of him so it did not seem so overwhelming. Then I broke our day up into short fifteen-minute learning blocks that sometimes didn't look like traditional learning at all. Each success during those short lessons brought greater results and confidence to explore more things that once perplexed him. For instance, we solved a math problem together and then I had him solve one, or I did a step in the problem and then had him do the next step. In his literature books, I had him read a few sentences and then we talked about what he thought. He remembered the short snippets of information better than full assignments. This back and forth method helped build his confidence and self-esteem, and soon enough we saw the quantity of work increasing as well. The whole process was labor intensive, but Larry and I resolved that *any* work he did this year would be an improvement over what he was able to do in public school. We had to continually remind ourselves that he was missing huge chunks of basic knowledge to start with, and progress would be slow and steady, and may take far longer than we hoped or expected. Some days were frustrating when it felt like we had reviewed the material for the hundredth time, and Patrick still wasn't getting it. Other days, we made huge strides.

Both of our children were thriving and we saw and shared in their successes every day. Our son was smiling again and pulling books off of shelves for the sheer pleasure of exploring them. Our daughter was blossoming too. She dove into learning and found workbooks enthralling, and free art time a delight. Her happy-go-lucky nature made our days easy and care-free.

Beverly Burgess

Larry and I found various games on special education websites that could help Patrick learn. They were much more entertaining than full-on book lessons, that were dry and boring. *Brain Pop (www.brainpop.com)* and anything to do with science were his favorite. Homeschool resources on the internet really exploded in those early years, and Morgan found sites like *Reading Eggs (www.readingeggs.com)* and *Starfall (www.starfall.com)* great fun. The local homeschool groups were a tremendous resource to us as well. There were parents in the group who had been homeschooling their different learner kids for years, and were very reassuring and forthright. They were helpful in finding curriculum and in letting us borrow texts and other resources before we purchased anything. One of the moms from the group said to me, "A curriculum won't solve any learning difficulties — it's just a tool. The main thing is just to keep plugging along. There will be good days and not so good days. Get used to it."

We knew this, but it was good to hear from others that what we were experiencing was just a stepping stone.

Part II The Practical

You Can Homeschool

If I'm being completely honest, I was terrified to the bone to homeschool my children, and I'm still terrified every single day. I was fearful that I would forever damage our kids or worse, ruin any chance of our kids contributing to society in any meaningful way. In the beginning days, I was unsure of what to teach and how to do it, but other parents reminded me that we are, and always have been, our child's first teacher. Homeschooling is no different than potty training, or helping our child to walk. Each requires patience, perseverance and knowing when to ask for help. Don't assume that you will know all the answers as you begin. I struggled a lot during the first year and asked tons of questions when we were out on playdates with other parents and children, and posted frequently to online groups.

Things like lesson plans, and planning out our day and even choosing curriculum, seemed such a daunting task, and one I had to get right from the very start. I wondered how I would ever teach subjects that I was not well versed in, or never took myself. Larry and I worried if the kids were learning enough, and sometimes worried they were learning too much. What if there was a subject we didn't feel comfortable teaching or didn't have resources for? What if our kids were smarter than us? Our heads swirled with thoughts of failure and the colossal undertaking that lay ahead of us. All of it felt overwhelming and not manageable at all.

I have always believed in the 3 R's, reading, writing and 'rithmetic.' But I found that my philosophy about even the three R's has changed a lot over the years. My goals have drastically switched from subject and course completion, to things like world views, perseverance, love of learning, and adaptability. Qualities that build character like kindness, compassion, honesty and integrity, respect for others, and respect for self — are far more important than whether kids can figure out the Pythagorean Theorem.

One of my public school teacher friends reminded me that all children (and adults too), have gaps in their learning. Children will be more successful with some subjects, topics or studies than others. Some things will come easily and others will be a struggle, just like kids in public and private school, and just like adults. Why do we make it okay for adults to have gaps in their learning, but expect children to know and learn everything during their years in school?

Over coffee one day, a local homeschool mom reminded me that if we are unsure of a topic or struggling with it ourselves, that tutors, online classes, homeschool cooperatives, other homeschooling parents, and all sorts of free help is available at our fingertips. She also reminded me that sometimes the chosen curriculum is not a match, and switching it up might prove beneficial to both the parents and child's understanding of a topic.

Larry and I were products of public school education when learning took place in a room from 9 to 3 during the day. It was hard to get out of the mindset, that there was learning happening at all hours of the day, and not just at prescribed times. New concepts or topics took far less time to teach and understand than they did in public school. The kids were not occupied with busy work or waiting for the rest of the class to catch up. They weren't moving from one class to another, or waiting in the lunch line, or for a stall in the

Out of the Box Learning

bathroom to open up. Our homeschooling was seamless and efficient.

Many of us who have been raised attending public schools, have hung on to the belief that knowledge is concrete — a boxed set of facts that can be memorized only during school time. But learning is fluid and shifting for all people, not just kids. The idea that knowledge is only obtained after twelve or more years of school, is an antiquated way of thinking.

During our first months of homeschooling, Larry and I tried to make sure that our kids kept up with the kids in public school, at least as far as topics and subjects covered. I browsed my local districts website, reviewed their scope and sequence and what curriculum they were using, just to be sure we stayed on track. As the year went on, it became less important to follow what the public school kids were doing, and more important to find things that interested us, and to work at our own pace. Initially, I patched together a hodge-podge of texts, internet sites and unit studies in addition to the boxed curriculum, to get us through a few months. As I watched my children each day, I realized how unique and individual each one of them really was and how each of them learned very differently.

Another thing that I had to get out of my head was that homeschooling should like public school at home. At first, I decorated our homeschool space to look like a public school classroom, thinking that's what the kids needed in order for learning to happen. This was a huge mistake but eventually, you figure it out when the kids have no interest in the poster about nouns that you just hung on the wall. We also didn't need a designated classroom or space for learning in our home even though we had one. The kids much preferred to bring their work to their bedrooms, couch or kitchen table. Our homeschool room contains the mess of all things you acquire for homeschooling, but the kids rarely use the room to complete the work unless they need the computer. Still, it's nice to be able to find everything we need in one spot. Books aren't missing as frequently either, since they have a designated spot on the shelf and are seldom lost now. It's also nice to be able to keep the huge amounts of homeschooling supplies out of the main area of the house and behind closed doors when company comes. Even if you don't have a designated space, find a cabinet or storage box for all of your homeschool supplies. It makes life so much easier when you can find what you need. Don't be surprised if you end up with bread-mold growing experiments on your dining room table, or kid's art work taped all over your glass patio doors. It seems once kids are home, homeschooling takes over the house. No matter how hard you try for it not to, it will still happen because homeschooling is such an extension of life.

Through the years, my kids have been at various grade levels of work. They might excel and move three grades ahead in the sciences, yet need more time to master math concepts. We've had some children in our homeschool group, that by public school standards have been late readers. But through patience and direct on-on-one instruction from the parents, these kids blossomed when they were ready. Not one adult or college poses the question, "At what age did you learn to read." Keep that in mind when you start to obsess about college and your homeschooler, and whether you are doing the right thing for your children.

Because of the individualized nature of homeschooling, late readers are not considered a handicap, as they might be in a traditional school setting. Schools rely on grade level-based instruction being kept at a certain pace all year long. In contrast, homeschooled late readers learn by utilizing other means, like working directly with siblings, computer games, audio books, peer groups and parents, homeschool cooperatives, and participating in the world around them. Since the homeschooler is not labeled as "slow" or put into the slow reading group, their self-confidence and self-esteem does not suffer. The children are then able to view reading as an enjoyable activity. Late readers do just fine, if they are not shamed and stressed to read oro reach the performance level of that of their peers or designated grade level.

Out of the Box Learning

Larry and I watched our kids intently and talked often about their learning patterns. Sometimes the kids took six weeks (or longer!) to learn long division or a new concept, when it may only be covered for one week in public school. Some days mastery came easily, and other days we went through material at a snail's pace. We spent as much time as needed with our children to help them master the concept, rather than complete a chapter just because we were on a timeline, bound to calendar dates, or because the lesson plan said we should. In fact, we weren't obligated to follow the public school calendar, or any topics covered in public school, so we could set up any schedule that worked for us, and cover any material that interested them. The reality was that even if long division took six weeks to learn, the kids spent less time on other chapters and concepts that were more easily understood. At the end of the day or the school year, their learning all evened out and we had to be okay with the ebb and flow of the process.

Homeschooling is hard work and takes an absolutely committed parent to facilitate this journey. It is not for everyone. In my coaching work, some parents readily admit that they don't really want to homeschool, but feel trapped or haven't researched alternative educational options. A few parents have told me that they don't really enjoy being with their kids, and have asked if there were other parents available to homeschool their kids.

I have advised some families not to homeschool when the commitment to relationship and the children's education, was just not there. It's a matter of self-awareness. Just like all things in life, you have to find what works for your family. While I can sing homeschooling's accolades all day long, it may not be a fit for your family and that's okay. Families should not feel guilty in either homeschooling, or using public or private education. What I do ask is that you've researched all choices thoroughly and aren't making decisions based on myths, hearsay, or someone else's experiences. If you've called homeschooling groups, contacted a coach, talked to other homeschooling parents, searched the internet, attended some homeschooling events and done everything you can, and still feel homeschooling isn't a match for your family —be settled with that decision. You have done your homework and made the best decision you can for YOUR family. Some homeschoolers, have kids both homeschooled and in public school. The only decision to make regarding your children's education is whether it is the right fit for YOUR family or child.

There is no shame in attempting to homeschool and realizing it's just not your cup of tea. Neither should the decision to stop homeschooling, be considered a failure. Life circumstances change and sometimes kids return to public school. I would stress however, that if you want homeschooling to work for your family and are struggling, to seek out the help of other homeschoolers or homeschool groups, or a consultant for support. I would also recommend that you not hold your first year of homeschooling as the high bar of all future years. The first year is about finding your way and getting your feet wet. Your first year will likely not resemble all future homeschool years. The only failure in homeschooling is not asking for help when you need it.

A few parents have told me that they didn't want to be home all day with their kids, or that their kids drive them crazy during school vacation weeks. If you are home all day trying to homeschool your kids, never to see the light of day or other people, reconsider your daily schedule. Homeschoolers are out of the house more than they are home. I am more excited when we have a day at home to finally work through lessons, or a project that may need a little more attention.

I have also coached parents who have not been able to clearly define their own goals and parenting styles; not fare well with homeschooling. Almost all unsuccessful homeschooling attempts that I see, are not because the parents weren't capable of teaching, or that the children weren't learning, but because of lack of goal setting.

Sometimes homeschooling doesn't work out because of a parent and child's learning style mismatch, or because of different expectations from the parent and child. Your children need to be able to take direction from you, and that includes during homeschooling. I tell every new parent I meet that homeschooling is really 99% parenting. Changing curriculum or the method of homeschooling doesn't always fix homeschooling struggles. Most times I see parents give up when homeschooling had little to do with their success or failure in the first place. Most times it has more to do with parenting and the unmet expectations in the homeschool setting. First time homeschoolers sometimes have an idyllic view of what homeschooling will look like. We all have had that when we started.

I met a local mother and father for a homeschool consult. They had been homeschooling for about six months, and things were going terribly. I asked them about their day and homeschool structure, and if they were getting out to see other homeschoolers and exploring the world. Then we moved on to talk about parenting styles and their expectations. When I asked them to describe themselves and their child to me, they told me that they both had college degrees and put a high emphasis on academics, but their child was a free spirit. They didn't have very many rules or expectations when it came to responsibility around the house, but they expected their child to adhere to the work given to him, and he often refused. This child was receiving mixed messages from the parents. The parents style of homeschooling was very academically oriented and the child's "free spirit," was a complete mismatch to the parent's expectations. The battle became constant because of the differing needs and inconsistent expectations.

Either the child will need to change or the parent will, if homeschooling is going to be successful. Since kids rarely change who they are, I recommended that the parents re-evaluate their expectations and at the very least, how they were going to continue to homeschool if their expectations didn't match with their child's. Yet, finding middle ground, is also doable. Ultimately, these parents were unable to alter their expectations and a few short months later, re-enrolled their child in public school.

Beverly Burgess

In my home, I was clear from the very first day with my children that mom and dad were the teachers and that all of our jobs, was to do the very best we could in our learning and all that we did. We also made clear what the word truancy meant and that if children, whether homeschooled or in public school, refused to go to school or do "schoolwork," that the parents and kids could be in trouble with the law. Parents need to set the expectation in the homeschool just as they do for other areas in the household, whether it's curfews or chores, while keeping in mind the spirit of the child. Whatever style of homeschooling you choose, whether is a free-spirited unschooling mindset or strictly academic, be sure your kids are getting consistent messages in all areas. Setting goals and expectations early in the homeschool process saves a lot of difficult conversations later on. I highly recommend that parents and children set the goals and expectations for their family and homeschooling together. When kids have an active role in their own homeschooling, the outcome is always wonderful and reachable!

Homeschooling and Public School

On several occasions I've been asked if I'm against public school. The answer is yes and no. I believe our public school teachers are loving and dedicated, but are no longer allowed to use their creative energy to teach in effective and innovative ways. They are no longer trusted by state or federal governments with the education of our children. Teachers are held accountable based on how well children test, as if their teaching were the sole factor in children's learning. They are penalized and removed from teaching, if a certain percentage of their students don't score in an acceptable range on standardized testing. Schools are threatened with the withdrawal of federal and/or state funding if a minimum score is not reached, or if schools are considered underperforming. We punish teachers as we do our students — with shaming, blaming and demerits. The system itself, not our teachers, has become so deeply flawed, that it's hard not to get discouraged at what is now considered learning.

I've also been accused of bailing on public education by pulling my kids out of, or not choosing public school. Parents and teachers have told me that it's my responsibility to change the system and to stick it out until things improve. No, it's really not. When my kids were in public school, I was active with special education, was present for every meeting for my child, attended school committee meetings, volunteered at every event and sold every cookie, popcorn tin and tchotchke for their fundraisers. Larry and I were directly involved in our children's education, yet we were still unable to change the system for our children or any others, despite being actively involved in and outspoken about it. We tried for years to make changes to the system.

But how long should I keep my child in a failing system that doesn't serve him on any level? Would any of us as adults keep a job or stay in a college course that didn't serve our needs, or that reduced us to tears on a daily basis? Of course not! We'd transfer or find an alternative. My child's education is important to our family, but how long must I wait it out, give it another try, or subject my child to something that is not a match for their learning? My children and their education is my priority. I could not let the fear of no longer being a part of the system, hold me back from seeking alternatives to educating my children. The fear with many homeschoolers is that no matter how terrible their current educational choice may be, removing their children from the system feels like the rug and all support systems are pulled out from under you. It is a frightening leap of faith to take.

Thinking back to my own public school experience I would say it was adequate, and I assumed that it would be equally adequate for my children. Adequate. Good. Okay. Not spectacular or life changing, or even challenging or exciting, but adequate. I wanted more for my children.

Words like grit and rigor, which have become catch phrases in modern day education reform, assume that kids aren't already trying hard, or their very best in all they do. It was what was assumed of Patrick; that his inability to perform as expected was because he wasn't trying hard enough, or that he wasn't determined enough to succeed. Grit, according the Merriam-Webster dictionary, is *mental toughness and courage*. Kids who are alternate learners, show their grit every single day when they show up, and try and try again. My child had more grit than any other child I knew and still was not succeeding.

Out of the Box Learning

Rigor is another word that is used frequently in public school circles. Merriam-Webster Dictionary defines rigor as *"the quality of being unyielding or inflexible,"* and *"the difficult and unpleasant conditions or experiences that are associated with something."* That sounds absolutely awful doesn't it? Don't we want education and learning to be the opposite of that? I prefer joyful and adventurous, rather than unbending and inflexible for my children.

When Patrick was in public school they used punishment and coercion to entice him and the other students to learn. Think about the *wall of shame* that was discussed earlier. The system saw a need to provide motivators to get him to learn — like grades, tests, honors, and gold stars. The problem was, he was already motivated, but when he could not perform as the district wanted, they gave him red zones, took away his recess, compared him to high performing children, and shamed him into learning — in hopes of having a better outcome.

To meet student's needs in public schools, learning techniques like differentiated instruction are used. Differentiated instruction or DI, is a framework for teaching that involves providing alternate learners with different methods to learn by. However, if DI were truly possible in the public school setting, you would need to be able to change at least one of three things in any lesson — 1) The content of the lesson, or what is being taught. 2)The process, or how it is taught or, 3) The end result or outcome or, how students prove their learning. Giving a child a different worksheet at a pre-arranged level, lower than where the student "should" be, is not really differentiated instruction. The student has been essentially, regrouped into a different standardized outcome.

It is not possible to have both individualized instruction and standardization. You cannot both individualize, and standardize a child's learning. Standardized learning requires that the content, process and result is the same in every instance, for every child. Schools require that all three items be in place and adhered to, in order to effectively measure content, delivery and progress. All three criteria are measured against how well or poorly students do compared to other students, rather than their own goals. Homeschooling is the opposite of standardization and provides direct, individual learning through changes in content, process and results. No two children are expected to work through the content, process, or to arrive at the same result at any time.

Infants thrive on individualized learning and develop so quickly because they try and try again without fear of being told not to experiment. It is why they choose to read the same book over and over again, or fill the bucket with balls, only to empty it and refill it again with great determination. All children will try until they have gained enough information or mastered the skill. They stop trying when they are punished for not getting it right. Instead of seeking out an answer or asking more questions, they wait until someone gives them the right answer, or tells them they are doing it the right way, or the expected way.

Homeschooling, or one-on-one tutoring has always been recognized as a superior method of teaching children. Customizing curriculum and instruction to each child's strengths, limitations, learning style and interests — is a proven way to maximize educational progress like no other method can do. Rather than a cookie cutter, one-size-fits-all approach for twenty to thirty children in a classroom, home education honors the individuality, creativeness, learning pace, and spirit of each child.

Homeschooling works so well because there is no pressure to perform to anyone's standards, but the child themselves. There is no unnatural separation of subjects as found in institutional learning. We may indeed teach math or spelling, but homeschooled kids are free to explore and expand on any topic. Text books used in the homeschool setting, may become more of a guide rather than an instructional manual. With the world at our fingertips how can we choose anything but being non-standard!

Educationese

A parent came to see me and was quite distraught. She was sullen and crying over her child's public school experience. Her sad and formerly vibrant, twelve-year-old now disliked school, cried every morning and didn't want to go back. Her daughter, who once loved violin, now found no time to practice because of a heavy academic work load. Additionally, the music program at the school had been recently defunded, and kids were making fun of her for being in the school orchestra. Extracurricular activities like music and art, while very important to this child, were no longer considered important in such an academic environment. They were separate learning experiences outside of the academics that were dissolved for "real learning," to take place.

As I spoke with this parent we talked about the need of schools for order, regularity and compliance in their day. Grade succession must be in order. Testing, and subjects studied must all be in order. Compliance must follow order.

Standardization is built on the premise of showing a child's deficiencies. Deficiencies in students are addressed with summer work, summer school, and online programs to bring a child up to the standard grade level of his or her peers. Just the opposite is usually expressed by the institutions, in that they proclaim that it shows the child's strengths. If that were true, schools would have not only remediation programs, but would highlight and provide programming for the strengths of a child and those that excel. Imagine if your child's school contacted you to say they tested your child, or that her teacher noticed that she has great musical ability. The school tells you that they would like to provide her with one-on-one music instruction, or bring in someone from the Philharmonic to hear her play, or enroll her in an advanced music class. Or maybe your child is showing a great interest in mechanics, and they would like to try her in an advanced engineering class, and set up an apprenticeship with a local naval base. What if children's abilities rather than what they could not do, were emphasized and explored?

Areas that children struggle with should also be provided for, and in a sense they are in public schools with extra testing and worksheets, and remediation for whole districts that are not up to par with the required mandated test scores. This is where the individualized instruction in homeschooling defeats all other methods when children need more time to blossom.

In homeschooling, curriculum is chosen by interest or skill level instead of a child's age, or expected grade level. Both children who are advanced, and those who need more instructional time, benefit greatly from this method. A child can move ahead in grade level when understanding is gained, and they can they spend extra time on areas of struggle until mastery is achieved. Answers and sometimes more questions, come later after a topic is fully explored, dissected and pulled apart. Only then can a child gain full understanding and relate it to the rest of their world.

Parents sometimes ask me how they will know if their children are learning, and if we need to test them to prove learning has occurred. Testing, to the extent it is done in public school, is unnecessary in homeschooling. A child's own self-improvement is a clear marker of progress. Parents can readily observe daily progress. We are with our children for extended periods of time and can identify strengths that can be built upon, as well as areas that may need work. Busywork, homework, and testing do not ensure that learning is happening. In many cases, when children are being tested, the information is memorized in order to pass the test. Remember "cramming?" It is doubtful that any of that information was retained, or would be remotely helpful for a person to succeed later in life.

My advice to parents is to get the "educationese" of public school out of your heads when you decide to homeschool. Put aside that language we are all used to hearing and adhering to. Create an environment and love of learning where all can enjoy the days as they pass by. Falling into the trap of learning inside a box does not benefit anyone, and doesn't work on any level of homeschooling.

How much of what we learned from our own days of schooling do we actually remember? Learning no longer happens just within the walls of a school. Public school used to be a necessity because there was no other way to learn. A teacher delivered the information and the children absorbed that information, and it was assumed that learning occurred. That is no longer the case as we are inundated with many new ways to learn about our world — tutors, the internet, community classes, apprenticeships, and the vast amounts of online learning that is being offered, are all options for learning. Colleges are even offering online classes and remote degrees. Students and parents are seeking out ways to get creative with their children's education, and are finding great joy in the process.

Why Homeschool?

Parents who are just beginning to explore homeschooling, find comfort connecting with those who are already homeschooling, or who are more experienced in the process. The direct conversations offer reassurance and real life experiences, that gives the homeschooling parent the confidence to try a new educational path. Many homeschool groups host workshops for parents who have just started to homeschool, or are considering it. Homeschooling coaches are a great resource as well if you need more support or just don't know where to turn.

The reasons for homeschooling are as varied as one might imagine. Many of the reasons parents share for homeschooling are:

- Unhappiness with increased use of teaching to the test and standardized testing in public school.
- Dissatisfaction with public school methods and atmosphere.
- Children who are advanced are not challenged and must remain at grade level regardless of learning capability.
- Children who need further instruction are left behind regardless of mastery of skill.

- Ability to use a wide range of teaching methods and approaches based on child's individual needs.
- Ability to customize or individualize the learning environment for each child.
- The desire to enhance family relationships between children, parents and among siblings.
- To provide social interactions with all groups not just age or grade related peers.
- To provide a safer environment for children and youth, away from physical violence, drugs and alcohol.
- To provide a more well-rounded education with exposure to real world problems and problem solving.
- Ability to tap into community resources with ease and without restrictions of public school day.
- Children have a vested interest in their own learning and education.
- The ability to pursue outside interests.

Parents long for deeper connections with their children, just as Larry and I did. A person I met at the park who did not agree with homeschooling, lectured me for over forty minutes that homeschooling parents were the "ultimate helicopter parents". Nothing could be further from the truth. Homeschooling parents give their kids wings to fly by exposing them to all kinds of opportunities. Our goal is not to manage what they learn, but to facilitate their journey toward learning.

Early in our first homeschooling year my children wanted to learn about ancient Egypt. We had plenty of books on Egypt and mummies, but sitting the kids in front a text and reading about Egypt seemed so boring to me, so I created a lesson plan about ancient Egypt instead. We spent our days at museums looking at the mummies and artifacts. We mummified dolls with white glue and torn bedsheets, and dehydrated chicken bones as we learned out ancient

Egyptian body preservation methods. The kids mixed their own natron, or desiccant — to help dehydrate the bones by blending salt, baking soda and flour, and used the scientific method to measure how many days it took to dry the bones. We made a sarcophagus out of clay, and wrote in hieroglyphics on the mummified doll for the burial procession. The kids made magnificent burial masks with dollar store purchases, lots of cardboard and papier mache'.

Each of them made an ancient Egypt folder filled with information about the desert biomes, the geography of Egypt, and wrote a story of what it was like to live during that time. They learned about the gods that were worshipped and watched a Netflix story on King Tut, and marveled at the scaled pyramids we built out of sugar cubes. Had we just read about Ancient Egypt from a text, it would have been a less memorable learning experience. The more valuable piece of those fun days was the time I was able to spend with my children. As they worked through each of their projects it gave me deep insight into their learning, and to the many alternatives to just textbook learning.

The Marriage Dance, Self-Care & the Mess

Marriage and partnership is hard work. My husband and I have witnessed many relationships crumble over time, and we've seen marriages shatter into broken pieces in an instant. Relationship work is not for the faint of heart. It demands a continuous reach toward one another in an ever challenging and changing world. There is no straight path, only measured steps that can get you to the finish line.

There are days — many days, when all you can do is sit in silence, remembering gentler days that didn't require so much of your heart, and soul, and energy. A true partnership in your relationship, in homeschooling, and even in sweeping the kitchen floor, is vital for success. Every turn, lift, carry and fall in the marriage dance, must have perfectly timed steps. I'm so grateful my husband and I are still reaching after twenty-six years together.

My best advice for new and seasoned homeschoolers is this: there are only two things you need to successfully homeschool your children; love and self-care. Beyond that, nothing else matters. That has been the most important lesson I have learned on this journey.

Homeschooling parents must have a love of learning, a love of family, a love of self and others, and a love of being inquisitive. They must be willing to provide self-care not only to themselves, but to nourishing new relationships, romantic and otherwise. It is important for single parents as well.

What I can tell you is that your marriage/partnership needs to come first, even before the children and before homeschooling. That doesn't mean that I don't love our children or wouldn't do most anything for them, or that homeschooling isn't a top priority for us. It just means that parenting and homeschooling, and life in general can sometimes suck you dry of energy and time, and leave little couple time. Couples (and those dating) need time to reconnect away from their kids and from homeschooling, in a space of mutual emotional and/or physical intimacy.

While sharing duties in homeschooling is wonderful, it is imperative that you be able to escape from the everyday responsibilities of parenting and work, whether out in the work force or at home. My marriage is integral to how I/we parent and how I homeschool. If my marriage is struggling and unhappy, my children and homeschool will undoubtedly be unhappy. Setting time aside for couple care is imperative. I am fiercely protective of our date nights. My husband and I both budget for and schedule our date nights at minimum, once a month. It is hardly ever at a five-star restaurant but time away from the house and children to share a meal or a glass of wine, or walk on the beach with your partner in quiet, is vital.

When money for date nights is short, we pack a picnic lunch and go to a park without kids, or spend some time at a local vineyard where we try wine tasting and listen to jazz for just a few dollars. We've attended free summer concerts and even lectures that we were both interested in. If there were months that money was very tight, we'd schedule a date night in. Send the kids to the grandparents' house for a night, or let them stay home if they are older. There is no guilt or harm with renting a movie, ordering pizza, making the kids popcorn and sending them to bed early. Retire to the bedroom

Out of the Box Learning

or back deck with a bottle of wine, and give the kids strict orders that they are not to disturb you under any circumstances. Don't knock on the door, don't fight, and don't make me come out of this room! An older sibling can certainly keep things under control for a few hours while the parents reconnect.

As a homeschooling parent, you will be with your children a lot, both in the home and in the car, and out at events. It's critical that you not give up your routines and things you loved prior to starting homeschooling, and that you continue with good self-care. If you went to the gym every day before you started homeschooling, or if you have weekly choir practice, be sure to continue those things which bring you joy and define you as an individual. If you don't currently have any hobbies, find some that don't include children, or homeschooling, or even your partner. The time alone is vital to your health and well-being.

Parents, and mothers in particular, should never feel guilty for needing a break or even taking a few hours to get together with other parents to rejuvenate themselves. Men are entitled to this time alone as well, but I make the point because women and mothers often end up the martyrs. We give up what is best for us and what fulfills us, because there is so much to be done and not enough time to do it. Who else will do it if mom doesn't?

Kids sometimes throw tantrums when mom leaves or when she returns home, or they don't want her to leave the house at all. Don't stand for it from anyone in the home. We give enough of our ourselves every single day to parenting, "spousing" (intimacy, tending to your spouse, paying bills, working, couple time, cooking, and anything that else that keeps a house/marriage running), and homeschooling. If you are leaving your family for a few hours to rest and refresh your soul and feeling guilty about it, you need to stop that immediately. You do not need anyone's permission, acceptance or guilt when you choose to take care of yourself, either in the moment or in the days that follow. In fact, you should run far away from those people or at the very least, begin these new, healthy practices right away. A walk in a park or on the beach each morning can become part of a daily routine, one that can be restorative for you to be your best self with your children and partner. Time alone is equally as important as time with your partner or children. I would say even more important. Use it wisely and never, ever give it up.

Single parents need breathing space too. If you can afford a babysitter for a few hours each week, it is money well spent. If your budget is tight, perhaps swap childcare with another homeschooling parent. Many are thrilled with this arrangement as it offers a playdate for the kids and a chance for the parent to get away for a few hours. Most parents are happy to have a few extra kids tag along on a field trip or park day. It keeps the kids occupied, creates a built-in play date and is sometimes less work for the parent. Playdates at our house are welcome. The kids are usually busy outside, and I get a few minutes to sit on the deck with a glass of lemonade. Or, I can take some time to actually clean up that messy house while the kids are being entertained by others and not underfoot.

If your homeschool group or community organization has drop off classes, take advantage of those as well, and go sit in a coffee shop with a good book or invite the other parents to join you. Homeschooling parents run a high risk of burnout from trying to do it all. Keep marriage time and self-care time, sacred. Never, ever, veer from things that will keep you healthy, happy and refreshed. Get rid of those things that don't honor your own self-care or worth.

Homeschooling is hard work and if your kids are home all day, your house is likely to look like a bomb went off. My husband and I initially struggled with the constant mess. Three kids were home all day, the sink was full of dishes, laundry was not folded, and the house was unorganized and cluttered. There was little evidence of me or the kids doing our part to keep things under control during the day. The kids' books, art projects, and various stages of science projects lined our counters and tables. My once balanced and healthy dinners became an endless stream of leftovers, crockpot meals and mac and cheese offerings. Muddy floors, dog hair furry carpets, and bathrooms that are scarier than a nuclear reactor, all became a part of our daily life.

It took almost a year to figure out a system of straightening and maintaining the disarray. Each day in the late afternoon the kids and I grabbed a basket and went through all rooms of the house, and gathered the items that didn't belong there. Then we'd do a second round through all the rooms and put everything back where it belonged. The books soon began finding their way back to the bookshelves, the art projects were moved downstairs for completion or drying, the science experiments were moved to a back kitchen counter, and the kitchen table was wiped down from the sticky handprints and food items.

To remedy the messiness, I began planning meals in the morning and having the kids help with the meal preparation at dinner time, and we started getting chores done before we began our homeschool day. The decluttering each day let me breathe and still feel like there was some semblance of my house still being under control. We still have to stay on top of the mound of dishes in the sink, and my kitchen floor is perpetually laden with dirt and spills. Those are things I have to live with and let go of. We can't do it all, and some days it all falls to pieces, and other days it's a well-oiled machine. Swish the toilet, hang fresh towels, put on a pot of coffee and enjoy your company, or partner's homecoming without worrying about what your house looks like. It is likely your kids had a wonderful productive day and being creative is messy business.

The S Word

The S Word — Socialization. The socialization myth concerning homeschoolers has been around since the 1970's and for some reason, refuses to die. Ask a homeschooler about socialization and you might just see some eye rolling or heavy sighing. To this day on message boards and forums and in articles about homeschooling, it is still the number one question and concern that is expressed, right after the curriculum question. No other part of homeschooling has brought more attention, examination, and criticism than socializing our children.

    Authors of articles and blogs tell the world that homeschooled children will be socially inept or weird, or that we have to try harder to socialize our children when they are homeschooled. That is likely true if you live in an area where your household supplies have to be flown in by airplane, otherwise, get the thought of how your children will be socialized out of your head. The reason we homeschool is not so we can lock our children away from our community to be raised in isolation, but so that they can be part of the community and interact with people of all ages. The stereotype of secluded homeschoolers who never leave their kitchen table or home, does not fit in today's world of homeschooling families. The opportunities for being active in the community are too wonderful to not take advantage of them.

Socialization seems to be a problem with adult expectations, rather than a problem with children. What seems normal to most adults, is that socialization takes place within the walls of a school. Statements about lack of socialization also imply that parents do not have enough social skills to teach their children, or will be incompetent in that teaching. It implies that we are capable of socializing them up until about age five, but not when they are school age. Most socialization skills are learned from parents and our community throughout life. Socialization is not restricted to a certain age group — such as in the school age years, or even within the confines of a building, or certain time of day. Rather, it is a lifetime process and only learned by interacting and engaging with many different people of all ages and stages of life.

Socialization happens everywhere; at the bank, on the playground, at concerts and amusement parks, and at libraries. Forced association that happens in the public school setting, is not socialization, and one might argue that homeschoolers are better able to handle the world, because of their exposure to it.

Socialization is a mostly organic process that kids will learn just by observing their world and by modeling those around them. Parents have asked me, "How will my children learn to: (insert any of the following) raise their hands, sit in a circle, stand in line, or listen when spoken to?" I've often responded with, "In the deli line, at Disneyland, at story time in the library, and we teach our children manners and model appropriate behavior."

Socializing on the other hand, is a choice. Socializing, or to mingle, is very much a choice that should be strictly in the hands of the child. Playdates are great to schedule, but watch your child's interactions. If playdates are stressful or just not a match for your child and their personality, don't continue them just for the sake of getting in that all important socializing. I am happy to introduce my children to others who share similar interests, but who they choose to make friends with is strictly up to them. Just as adults choose our own friends, children should also be given that privilege. This is not to suggest that parents shouldn't intervene if playdates become dangerous or stressful. It is only meant to suggest that kids have chemistry with other children, just as adults do and know who they "click" with. Certainly parents need to get their kids out in the world, but be cautious of over extending yourself. Socialization, being social and socializing, all look different to different children.

What most parents are asking when they ask about socialization is, "Will my child have friends?" I'd like to answer an unequivocal yes to that, but kids may or may not have friends and homeschooling usually has nothing to do with that. The best we can do is provide opportunities for our children to click with other children and adults. It is commonplace to see homeschooled children interacting, communicating and playing, not only with children of their own age group but with people of all ages. My own children see no difference in speaking to an adult about their planetary studies, then speaking to children at the playground about those same planets. From babies to elderly, homeschooled kids are usually comfortable speaking to a variety of people.

When my son was almost four years old, we were at the deli counter waiting for our number to be called. The store was particularly busy this day, and Patrick occupied his time by counting the packages of rolls in front of the counter until he caught sight of a pregnant woman. He went right up to her and put his hands on either side of her belly and pushed his mouth on her shirt and said, "Hey! Baby, can you hear me?" The mother smiled and rubbed Patrick's head as he continued with his line of questioning. The crowd moved back and made room for my son who was now in a circle and the center of attention.

"Are YOU having a baby? My mom's having a baby too." We were indeed expecting a baby, but we were adopting. I was clearly NOT pregnant as the crowd looked at me and mulled over my lack of baby belly. "'Cept she isn't having my sister through her 'gina," he said. "She's coming on a airplane and she has black hair. Do you know what color hair your baby has? I bet it will be brown. Do you have other babies at home? I don't. I have a dog and two cats. They sometimes poop on the floor and have stinky farts too. I hope my new sister doesn't poop on the floor," he chattered on.

When the pregnant mom turned her attention to the deli counter, Patrick began chatting with an older man and his wife and when they left, he moved his conversation to another child about his age and talked about his light-up sneakers. Clearly, my son had no issues with socializing or socialization. I, on the other hand was wishing for a somewhat less social child.

When we consider socialization and socializing, we should also give thought to quantity versus quality. How much social interaction do children need? The answer is difficult and very individualized. Just like adults, some children thrive in smaller groups of only a few kids and others prefer larger crowds. The reality is that children's needs may change on a daily basis just as they do with adults. My oldest son needed much time alone to rejuvenate and refresh. While he enjoyed being with other people, he also was quite comfortable being with himself and preferred time to explore his own interests.

Homeschool field trips are often great learning opportunities. While field trips add enrichment to any curriculum, they don't usually provide much opportunity to socialize — yet this is often the first place where new homeschooling parents think socialization and socializing occurs. Most times, field trips offer a great place to learn about a particular study area or topic, but there is not usually space or time for kids to get to know one another. This is usually due to how the program is set up, time constraints within the field trip, or because of the sheer number of children attending the field trip and the need to keep moving through the venue.

It is possible to schedule time after field trips for play dates at playgrounds and to make this known to the other homeschooling families. Play dates after field trips provide opportunities for the parents to get to know one another too. Snacks and lunches can be packed to share, or to keep kids hunger at bay. Since playdates seemed to happen in the spur of the moment, we kept a bag in our trunk filled with a change of clothes for each child, board games, paper and crayons, sunscreen, extra juice boxes, snacks, hats, a blanket and beach pails for impromptu playdates that we didn't want to pass up.

At a particularly busy time in my kids' homeschooling life, they were involved in 4H, karate, soccer, sign language, youth group, church classes, volunteering, babysitting and had been on several field trips and play dates at the playground. As I expressed my profound tiredness to a friend about our busy schedule, she interrupted with, "Aren't you worried that they won't be socialized?" No, I'm really not, I thought. Instead I just smiled and shrugged my shoulders. It wasn't worth the effort to explain it all again to this person, because even after all the activities out in the world, she still thought the kids weren't socialized or socializing, simply because they were not in school.

A word of advice to homeschooling parents; homeschooling does not fix social awkwardness. But what it does provide are ample opportunities for our children to work through social situations that might be difficult. Homeschooling offers many opportunities for practicing and getting it right without judgement or criticism. Instead of parents asking, "Is my child being socialized," perhaps the question should be, "Is my child empathetic, considerate and do they have a loving, giving heart? Do they feel safe coming to talk to me about anything? Do they treat others with compassion? Do they interact with a variety of people of all ages?" Socialization, rather than being an issue specific to homeschooling or even public school, is really a responsibility of parenting and of our society. Take the time to sit back and notice how much your children are already interacting with the world.

The Honeymoon Phase
& Deschooling

Just like in marriage, when parents decide to homeschool I remind them about the honeymoon phase. Many parents make the decision to homeschool, remove their child from public school and immediately start homeschooling lessons the next day. Fearful that any lapse in formal school work will result in their child falling behind academically.

During the first few months of homeschooling, things will likely go well. The curriculum has been chosen or borrowed from a friend, all the materials have been purchased and the first workbook completed, and everyone is still excited. The kids have settled into a routine and might be enjoying the freedom of more relaxed days. Then suddenly, the novelty wears off and they start missing their classmates and the routine of school, and are now faced with lots of time to fill on their own. The kids may begin to test boundaries and challenge the expectations you are giving them. They see you not as mother and teacher, but as someone who is struggling to find her own place in this new journey. There may be defiance and refusal to do any work asked of them. There may be regression in work that you know they have mastered, and there may be bouts of nagging in wanting to return to public school. Almost every homeschooling family I have known, goes through these stages.

Usually, about three to six months into homeschooling, parents contact me needing another consult, or post to social media begging for help. They've hit a brick wall or are crying; the kids are refusing to do any work, or someone ended up in the hospital due to illness, and their perfect schedule has been forever destroyed. There might even be a younger sibling that has needed much attention leaving little time for older kids, and suddenly little schooling has occurred and the parents are in a panic. A monkey wrench has been thrown into their imperfectly well-run homeschool machine, and they are at a loss and ready to quit.

It seems that no matter how hard they try, life is getting in the way of homeschooling and creating much stress for all. The parent who is responsible for teaching is frustrated and telling me it isn't working out, that their kids are falling farther behind, and that they are considering sending them back to public school. Rest assured, I have heard this hundreds of times and most times it works itself out.

The key to a successful transition from public school to homeschooling, lies with the parent, not the child. Parents who have pulled their child from public school have witnessed years of them struggling or even falling behind. The child may have had a less than stellar public school experience, yet homeschooling is not living up to anyone's expectations either. New homeschooling parents sometimes feel an urgent need to do better and to bring their children up to grade level with publicly schooled kids, especially if their children have fallen behind. I too, thought the same thing when I brought my son home from school. I felt like I had to make up for the lost years in public school, and everything my child lacked, must be corrected at once.

New homeschoolers tend to start homeschooling as soon as they withdraw their child from public school. They find any and all curriculum they can get their hands on to make up for the lapses in

Out of the Box Learning

learning. I was no different. While we pulled our oldest child out of public school after he completed the year, we dove right into homeschooling as soon as September rolled around. I should have given us all time to move away from the requirements of public school, far longer than just the summer months. My son, having been so damaged and defeated from public school, started to cry when I asked him to complete a single math problem. It took several weeks of my reassuring him that he wasn't going to fail the assignment if he wasn't able to complete it. The truth of the matter was, that he couldn't complete it. He couldn't complete much of any the work I gave him.

I had to completely rethink what I was doing and what my goals were for him. My goals were not for him to complete the next problem, question or workbook page, but for him to regain his love of learning, to build up his confidence, and for me to provide the tools he needed to succeed in a way that was meaningful for him. Completing any assignment would have to wait. It was almost a full year of homeschooling before he could finish a workbook page. As a parent that was a hard pill to swallow, especially when friends who had kids in the public school system looked at that inability, and assumed the cause of his falling behind was due to homeschooling him. I felt like I had to prove that I COULD homeschool him and make him learn, or else I would be a failure too.

When parents are withdrawing their children from the public school system, I always recommend a long period of deschooling. Formerly public schooled children need sufficient time to decompress from the public school experience. They need even more time to rediscover their creativity and explore things that may have been discouraged in their past experiences.

Some of the homeschoolers I've met who are acclimating themselves to homeschooling and deschooling, have no idea what they are even interested in. When I ask them, they tell me that they are good at math or science. "Yes," I say. "That's a subject you do well with, but what are you interested in?" Most of them cannot answer me because they have had little time to explore deeper interests other than those subjects required by school. Even extracurriculars become something to place on their college transcript rather than a love of learning. Homeschooling allows ample time for exploring all things that interest a child, not just the academic subjects.

Public school tells us that kids have regression in their learning, and in what they remember academically due to the long summer break and gap in learning time. The summer slide, they call it. I have never experienced this phenomenon with homeschoolers since all that we do is learning. Those homeschoolers who take long breaks during the summer or throughout the typical school year, experience very little backslide in their learning because they are so invested in it. If skills are forgotten, they are easily reviewed just as we do for adults in their professional and personal lives. When homeschoolers learn, it melds seamlessly into all of life. Learning is not based on a particular season, or because of mandatory attendance. Nor does learning stop when we leave a building.

The joy of homeschooling is that we are not bound by a calendar or, even which particular days during the week we choose to homeschool. Many homeschooling parents choose to create a schedule of four days out of the week, and use the fifth day for activities like music, sports, cooperative classes or even an academic class outside the home. Still others will homeschool on weekends, or in the evening due to work schedules. Whatever you choose to do, allow much free time and space to deschool and decompress. When the honeymoon phase comes to an end and it seems like you won't make it through another homeschooling day, take long walks in the woods, swim, meet new homeschooling friends and play. Meet some parents for coffee while the kids entertain themselves. Explore topics and choose some that you are interested in rather than what you think should be covered in a subject.

At every turn, re-evaluate your goals and remember why you chose homeschooling.

The Naysayers

Over the years I've heard from naysayers, or people opposed to homeschooling —that I've made a terrible decision in homeschooling my kids. Naysayers are the ones who are vocal, either directly or indirectly, about your ability or decision to homeschool. Their comments may be snide remarks or blatant comments during a family gathering. Those used to the public school mindset may voice concerns that the appropriate place for children is in a school environment, where professionals are trained in teaching children. The naysayers tell us that homeschooling will damage our children, and that it will make them weird, or unable to participate in society. My kids are already weird — in the best way, and homeschooling has nothing to do with it!

There is always the rare uncle, or dentist even, who will feel a need to quiz your child not only on academics, but will also compare them to public school kids. I usually cut these conversations off to the best of my ability and ask, "What is your concern about our homeschooling?" Family gatherings can create some awkward moments too if relatives continually quiz your children, or question your reasons for homeschooling. Family members and others may be vocal about homeschooling since they likely know little about it, or they might have heard the familiar stereotypes of homeschooling and assume that all homeschoolers fall on that spectrum. I usually answer with a light-hearted and to the point, "Gee, we came for Christmas dinner and family time. Next time let me know we'll be quizzed and I'll bring our Jeopardy game so we can all play!"

As you gain confidence in your homeschooling, you will learn to tell the difference between naysayers and those that are truly interested in homeschooling. I don't waste my time explaining to naysayers about homeschooling. They don't get it, aren't going to get it and will counter point you on every turn. They may drag you into long debates and sometimes feel a need to defend their own child's public or private school education. The conversation can be redirected by offering, "I'm glad you are satisfied with your educational choice. Homeschooling is working great for us as well." Then change the subject.

Homeschooling gives you a thick skin, and eventually the comments will likely roll off your back. Relatives, virtual strangers, acquaintances and those who don't know of any other way to educate children, may not be in favor of homeschooling, may have misconceptions about what really happens in the homeschool setting, or even what the educational outcome of child will be. It's fine to correct the misconceptions and myths, but don't spend time defending your decision to homeschool. You are making the best decision for your family and that is no one else's choice or decision, but your own.

Do I believe that homeschooling is superior to public school? For my family, yes but not for every family. Every family situation is unique and should be honored as such. As homeschoolers we have more opportunities in the community, a more well-rounded education, our kids are far more independent in their thinking, are more creative and love learning. The homeschooled kids I know are more willing to try, willing to make mistakes and try again when it comes to their learning.

Out of the Box Learning

It's best to take opinions and "expert advice" with a grain of salt. Then do what your heart calls you to do, and what you feel is right for your family. Most homeschooling advice given is based on the one family, or one experience of the naysayer, and they are likely to base everything they know about homeschooling on that one experience, whether it was good or bad. Usually it is a bad experience and they will go on to tell you how your children will be unwise, unprepared for the real world, and sometimes even become serial killers or mass murderers. Yes, someone actually said that to me. Naysayers are stuck in their own story and will likely not be open to hearing alternate outcomes when it comes to homeschooling. It is much like when you are pregnant and every pregnant woman has to tell you about their horrifying birth experience, bodily secretions, and how you should have a natural birth instead of a C-section. Their conclusion is that your choice was wrong for choosing a different path.

Naysayers tend to be vocal about their concerns, and however unfounded, can cause homeschooling parents to lose their confidence and question their choices. Sometimes answering them with a "Thanks for your concern. I'll take that under consideration," is all that is needed. The best way to deter naysayers is to be confident in your choices and to stand firm in your decisions.

I've also found it helpful, if you have a good relationship with your naysayer, to bring them to some homeschooling events. Most times they will refuse, but every once in a while they will decide to attend. I can tell you that always, they are surprised at how well-rounded homeschooled kids are, and are left flabbergasted at the choices and experiences available to homeschoolers today. They are also surprised at how unweird our kids actually are. One summer at our homeschool group's annual picnic, a very nice grandfather shook my hand and said he was completely mistaken about homeschooling. He went on to say that he was embarrassed about giving his granddaughter a hard time about it. Those are things I love to hear! This grandfather then went on to help homeschool his grandchild about the wars that he served in, and gave a really personal perspective and learning experience that couldn't have been acquired if the child had just read a text book. The grandfather also had a wonderful opportunity to build a relationship with his homeschooled grandchildren, and to spend more time with them.

It's also important to remember that those interested in learning more about homeschooling can occasionally appear as naysayers. One sunny Saturday while I was at the playground, a mom overheard me talking and asked, "But you can't possibly know how to teach algebra — how do you do that?"

"What is your concern or question about that," I asked.

"Well, I've been considering homeschooling for a long time but I have tons of questions. It all seems so overwhelming and I worry about teaching things I don't know a lot about."

I meet people like this all the time and it's a great opportunity to connect them to our homeschooling group, and get them started on their way. Most new homeschoolers are not even sure of the first questions to ask, and we need to remember that not every question asked is an assault on homeschooling. Ask your own questions for clarity if you think you have a naysayer in your midst. You just might be helping out a new homeschooler who is struggling with getting started like you once were.

When the naysayer is your partner or spouse, it can be much more difficult. I am fortunate to have a husband who is fully on board with homeschooling, but it wasn't always that way. When we (I) started homeschooling, the first several years felt like my husband tolerated what I was doing and went through the motions of my little hobby. But there was always the undertone of my teaching never being good enough, and public school re-enrollment looming over my head when he finally decided that I had failed our children enough. I spent every waking homeschool day making sure we had school work to show him, and versed the kids on what we did during the day so that they could answer him with something academic to show how we spent our time.

When you ask a public schooled kid what they did at school all day and they answer, "nothing," it's not a big deal. It has become the expected answer and it is assumed that they did do SOMETHING all day, because what else do you do in school? Parents don't flip out when a public school kid says, "nothing". But ask a homeschooled kid what they did and if they answer "nothing," you are sure to be criticized or condemned, because it implies they are lacking in their learning, or that "nothing" really does means that they did nothing all day.

Surely those homeschooled kids must have done something all day or have something to show for all of their hard work. There must be some dittos or piles of homework, or loose papers, or even a workbook that shows what they accomplished today, right? In the public school setting, those papers, and dittos, and homework indicate that learning happened. They tell us that work was completed and everything is as it should be. Homeschoolers may or may not have dittos or work to indicate learning, and that is really difficult for some people to wrap their heads around. How do I know you learned unless you have something to show for all the work you did?

It took my husband a long time to come around (six years or so) to homeschooling, but I persevered, and he finally relaxed when our first child went off to college. Recently he told me that those early years in homeschooling felt like a rebellion to him, that it didn't seem normal because everyone attended public school and it was all he knew. He had the same fear about socialization, the quality of teaching that I could provide, and whether our kids would be able to move on to higher education.

I felt like he had lost faith in me. After so many years of marriage, surely he knew that I didn't just jump into anything, and that I researched things thoroughly and presented a complete picture. He also knew that after fighting for services for my son for so many years, that my only goal was for him to succeed. But what I thought was best, and what he thought was best, were on opposite ends of the spectrum. He didn't trust me to ensure that our kids had all that they needed. He didn't trust us as a couple, that we could give our kids all they deserved and needed. It was rough. He needed to learn to trust our kids too — to know that they are awesome and inquisitive and miraculous. We had some very long talks about his fears and letting go of the old way of what education looked like.

The changes in standardized education and introduction of common core also changed his mind. I sent him numerous articles about the downfalls, politics and unproven methods of standardization, and we had long discussions about each of them. Larry read some essays from some public-schooled kids at the same grade level as our children, and was shocked at the misspellings, grammar inconsistencies, poor content, and high grades those kids received for subpar and below level work. I shared two essays with him, one from our children and one from a public schooled child and said, "Which one do you think shows more determination, accurate facts, creativity and clearer content?" We don't ever want to compare our children to others, but in this instance it was clear our children were doing just fine.

Larry also told me that when it came to homeschooling, my stubbornness paid off. I'm not one to give up easily and I persevered because I knew in my heart that homeschooling was the right choice for our family. Through the years, Larry has also been able to see the various learning styles of each of our three children. The oldest — sensitive and academic; the middle child — happy, carefree, inquisitive, athletic and will shut down if pushed too hard. It's why my husband does math with her in the evenings when she's at her best, and I am not. And our youngest — able to leap tall buildings in a single bound and a do-it-yourselfer. He is my engineer, and if he wants to build something he watches YouTube videos and makes it himself. He's constructed air raid sirens, created his own green screen, made movies and is gainfully employed at age twelve, doing lawn care and editing videos for an author friend for her personal business. He learned his editing skills on a program I know nothing about, nor did I show him how to use. He has his own YouTube channel with videos he has created that include cloning, voice overs and music. I'm amazed at his skill and determination in figuring out something he knows little about. None of it was taught in a curriculum, but rather through natural curiosity and a desire to learn.

Larry appreciated that those were skills our kids would never be able to learn if they weren't homeschooled. He sees the many opportunities that they have available to them every day from cooperative classes, to teen social groups, to managing their own physical education workouts. The social, enrichment and academic offerings available to our children are limitless. Be firm in your conviction to homeschool, in your choices for your family, and give things time to settle. The naysayers may become your biggest fans.

Homeschooling Mistakes

Our family has been homeschooling for over a decade and we've learned a lot along the way about what does and doesn't work. We have no regrets with homeschooling, only opportunities to learn and try again when things don't go as planned.

Here are some things to remember when you first start homeschooling.

1. Don't assume an expensive curriculum is the best.

There is no proof that an expensive homeschool curriculum will provide your child with a good, adequate, or even excellent education. The dollar amount you spend on homeschool material has no bearing on their educational outcome. Some homeschoolers spend tons of money on supplies and curriculum, and others spend next to nothing. Some do not use any textbooks at all, and instead find alternative ways to meet their educational needs. Libraries, free seminars, taking advantage of free museum openings or parks, can work equally as well as any curriculum.

Support and direct parental involvement, play a far greater role in learning, than a textbook does. Many homeschoolers (and public schools), have been duped and disappointed by the bells and whistles of a website, or well-known curriculum that touts educational success for homeschooled kids. Before you purchase anything, ask for feedback from other homeschooling parents or read online reviews and remember that what works for one child may not work for another. If you are able to download samples of the curriculum, or borrow texts from another homeschooler before you purchase — give it a thorough review and then decide. There are websites that sell or swap used curriculum where you might be able to find a cheaper price instead of spending full price on something you are not sure of. Do your homework to the best of your ability before purchasing.

2. Don't assume that the curriculum is the end all and be all.

Many parents who come to see me, change up curriculum when things aren't going well in their homeschool. This is a perfectly valid reason when your chosen curriculum is not matching up with your child's learning style. However, curriculum will not fix any homeschooling issues, and is not the only thing you should consider in your homeschooling. I have ditched curriculum before even using it or shortly thereafter, when it didn't match with our learning needs. In one instance, it was a science curriculum that was fraught with errors that I didn't notice until after I purchased. The curriculum only skimmed the surface of things I thought were important, so we tossed it aside in favor of something else. In another, the material in a language arts book that I purchased was dry and boring, so we chose something more engaging.

3. Don't try to re-create public school at home.

Trying to replicate public school at home almost always results in failure. Virtual schools can also be hard to navigate. Some are very much like public school at home in terms of hours and assignments that must be completed. My suggestion is to carefully research online virtual schools for tuition costs, and their reviews and recommendations, to determine if it is a match for your family. There are some well-done online programs, and some that simply recreate public school in the home, and charge large amounts of money in the process.

Some states require enrollment in umbrella or virtual schools, as part of their state laws in homeschooling. Parents should be very clear on what your personal goals for choosing homeschooling are, and be sure that you are choosing any avenue with great diligence and research. If your kids are following a traditional homeschooling path, remember that your homeschool doesn't need to resemble, in any shape, what public school looks like.

4. Be sure you are practicing self-care.

Self-care is vital to homeschool survival. Review the chapter on self-care again. It's that important.

5. Don't let the schedule take over.

Homeschoolers are busy. However, downtime is just as important as academics and events outside the home. If you are racing to the next class, the next sports event, the next thing on the list and feeling overwhelmed; you are likely doing too much. Try to allow at least one day a week or more when nothing is scheduled on the calendar. We schedule most of our activities out of the house on one or two afternoons a week, so that mornings can be reserved for studies. For other families, getting out of the house every day is the very reason they chose to homeschool. Do what is right for your family, but don't let the schedule take the fun out of learning or stress you out.

Homeschooling has the luxury of flowing with the family needs. A new family met with me for a consult several months back. The mom had a listing of the full day's activities planned out starting at 9:00 a.m. Subjects were divided into half-hour increments and color-coded for each child depending on grade level.

Out of the Box Learning

While this homeschooler's organizational and chart making skills were impressive, she had a recipe for disaster in the works. Life, homeschooling and learning doesn't work by a clock. I encouraged her to throw away the incremental study sessions and to try a more flexible plan that was not dictated by subjects or the clock.

There are no mistakes in homeschooling, only opportunities to learn.

State Homeschooling Requirements & Your Role

It would be difficult if not impossible to review all fifty states and their homeschooling requirements. I absolutely recommend connecting with a homeschooling group in your state. Homeschoolers and group leaders are well versed not only on federal and state laws, but on district policy and educational rulings. Depending on your state laws and requirements — you might have to report at the state, district or town level, which makes discussion on this issue even more difficult.

Even with strict state or district control, there has never been a study that shows any correlation between stringent homeschooling laws and successful educational outcomes in our children. NHERI — National Home Education Resource Institute, tells us that states with more restrictive homeschooling laws do not fare any better than those with few or no laws and in fact, those states with more educational freedom might do better because of the opportunities available.

State governments and local districts will often ask for more from homeschoolers than is required by law. Sometimes they will send information on how to create a duplicate version of public school at home. Some districts have asked us why we refuse to submit more information than is required by law, implying that homeschoolers had something to hide. Nothing could be further from the truth, and since we are in compliance with what the law requires — that should really be the only determining factor in our homeschooling journey.

Submitting more than is required by law is detrimental to other homeschoolers as well. The additional unrequired information becomes the expectation in our reporting, and sets the stage for future policy making that would be harmful to homeschooling in general. Homeschooling parents should educate themselves on homeschooling law so all are protected, and advocate for themselves when school committees or policy makers overstep what is required by law.

I have spent much time in front of school committees, at policy meetings, with superintendents, and have worked diligently to change policy to insist that homeschoolers rights are upheld. It's a hard battle, as most would like us to conform to their box of what they know education to look like.

Some things to research in your own state when beginning to homeschool are:

- Is there a letter or notice of intent to homeschool, that needs to be filed by a certain date?
- Is there a form letter or education plan you need to submit?
- To whom does it get filed with? (State, local district, superintendent, principal of your local school?).
- What end-of-year reporting are you required to file, if any? Narratives, portfolios, report cards, transcripts and even a full educational evaluation by a licensed teacher are required in some states.

- Is testing required? Must I send the results to the district? My state does not require homeschoolers to participate in standardized testing but many states do. Some states require testing at certain grade levels; some require the same standardized testing as public schools and others do not require any testing, or leave the method of testing up to the parent. Local homeschooling groups can help you with this as well.
- Are there attendance requirements? Some states require a certain number of hours or days to homeschool; some require that you follow the public school calendar, and still others have no oversight at all in that regard.
- Are there required subjects I must teach?
- Are their extra-curricular activities that must be included?
- Do you have to follow a specific curriculum?
- Can you withdraw a child from public school mid-year? What is the process to do that?
- Is any reporting required at all in my state?

  Be sure to connect with local homeschooling groups and become well-versed in your own state laws and policies. It is the best way to assure that you are in compliance with the law, and protecting your homeschooling rights.

Homeschool Groups & Cooperatives

Homeschool groups can be a great source of support to your family. Groups that might suit your family needs can be found in most every state, with many offering a multitude of services, from help finding curriculum to organized classes, to social groups, to support services. Do your research on any homeschool group you might choose to join. Many homeschoolers belong to more than one homeschool group, and use the benefits of all the groups to round out their homeschooling experience.

Some questions to ask before joining a group are:
- Is the group religiously affiliated or secular? Look for key words like welcoming and inclusive, or religious language. If you are unsure what the group is about, contact the group leader for clarification. Must you sign a statement of faith or adhere to it, if the group is religiously affiliated?
- Are you in agreement with the group's vision and mission?

- Is there a membership fee and what benefits does your membership fee include? Are their discounts for classes and other things for members?
- Does the group have bylaws and policies? How do they handle conflict?
- Is there a wide and varied way to connect with the larger homeschooling community?
- Are there homeschoolers in your area that you can meet regularly with, or do you need to travel a distance?
- Is the group mostly online support or are there in-person opportunities to meet?
- Has the group remained stagnant through the years, or have they grown and changed and provided new opportunities for homeschoolers?
- How many families are a part of the group? Is a small group or larger group better suited to your needs?
- Are they transparent with budgeting issues and board direction?
- Are there policies in place for safety like background checks, child safety policies, emergency procedures and reporting procedures?
- Are there newsletters, support seminars or social media groups that you can connect with?
- Does the staff arrange field trips/events and classes or is it up to individual members to arrange these things, or is it a combination of both?
- Are volunteer hours required to participate?

Groups that have been around for a while have the benefit of experience and wisdom of members who have been homeschooling for a long time. These members usually have lots of knowledge and insight on how to get kids through their schooling years and on to college. Groups that have been around for many years may also be stagnant. Check to see that new members are joining, and that members are volunteering to keep the group active.

Homeschool groups can be invaluable to homeschoolers. When our state didn't have what I was looking for in a group, I created my own. Whether large or small, secular or religious, be sure any group you join suits your own needs, and has what you are looking for to round out your homeschool.

Homeschool groups will inevitably have conflict. Parents won't always get along, kids sometimes disagree, and there will be disputes over policies and practices, and what's provided. It will happen even among friends. The important thing to remember about homeschooling groups is that they are run by volunteers who are balancing family life, homeschooling and sometimes work, just like you. They are giving up hours of their own time to support a group that they feel passionate about, and working hard to support the group as a whole. Recognizing the effort and time given by all volunteers, is a great way to show your appreciation.

Have a conversation with the leaders of the group if things are not going as you expected them to. Expressing displeasure about a situation or other member on social media, or in larger groups is always damaging to the group, and hurtful and disingenuous to the many members who volunteer their time for the benefit of your children. Try to see the intent of the person, and the root of what caused you to be upset. Was it meant to be hurtful, or is it simply a difference of opinion? Was it a serious problem that wasn't addressed adequately? Do you need to remove your child or yourself from the situation? Are you willing to clear the air to make things right, or would you rather hold on to the anger? Sometimes a group may no longer be a match for your needs and you might need to move onto another group, or no group at all. Be okay with knowing that groups change and grow just as your own family's needs change and grow.

Homeschool cooperatives can be a great asset for homeschooling families. Parents are usually responsible for planning, teaching and implementing the group's activities. Cooperatives are able to offer classes to a wider range of homeschooling children from just a few families to hundreds of families. They might be based on methods of homeschooling, or a certain subject, or whatever topic the parents are willing to teach. Teachers or facilitators of the classes may volunteer, or be paid for their services in a cooperative program. Most cooperatives have a volunteer component too, and may include clean up duty, or co-teaching, or helping to prep for a class. Many hands are needed to make these groups work efficiently and to provide quality classes.

Prices for cooperative classes can vary greatly from free, to hundreds of dollars, depending on what is offered and what parents are looking for. The benefits are that your child is attending a class and answerable to another adult besides yourself. Some parents also see that as a drawback, and prefer to choose what content or curriculum is available to their children in their own homeschool.

The homeschool cooperative program that my children attend is just one day a week, and offers anywhere from eighteen to twenty-five classes for all age groups. There are both academic and enrichment classes available, and parents can choose just one class or as many as their budgets will allow. Some cooperatives may require that you sign up for the whole day, a minimum number of classes, or pay for a whole year of classes, depending on what leaders and parents are available and how the cooperative is structured.

There are things to consider in a homeschool cooperative as well. Sometimes parents do not want to teach other people's children, and for programs that only offer full day classes, they can be very long days for children and parents. Well run programs can usually manage these small challenges, and often times a smaller cooperative or a more flexible schedule is a better fit.

Cooperatives can be a benefit for your children as it provides an opportunity to meet regularly with the same group of kids, helps parents provide structure in subjects that they might not have particularly strong skills in, and requires the children to be accountable for work from someone else. It also provides time for the parents to connect and get to know one another.

When deciding if a homeschool cooperative is right for you, consider the cost, time commitment, and whether you or your children will benefit from this type of structure.

Learning Styles

I don't spend a lot of time counseling new homeschoolers on learning styles when homeschooling. My own teaching and learning style is constantly changing, depending on the topic and what needs to be covered. My teaching style may change on how well my children are understanding or not understanding a lesson, and what kind of mood they are in that day.

There are online tests that children can take to determine what type of learner they might be. But the reality is that parents usually know what type of learner their child is, and how we learn changes depending on the material presented. Parents may not know the formal name for how their child learns, but can readily tell me if the child learns best by doing or seeing (visual learner), or feeling (tactile learner), or hearing (auditory learner), or a combination of these things.

Tactile learners do best by completing the task themselves. These children learn best when they take a hands-on approach to learning. These are the children who prefer using Legos to figure out math problems, who take apart old computer modems to see how they work and who prefer the messiest medium when working with art. These children need to feel and touch to understand.

Out of the Box Learning

Auditory learners learn best through the use of verbal communication. They have information revealed to them through written works, but in most cases, the information is not going to make sense until it has been heard. Auditory learners will benefit from creating recordings of the information that is to be taught. These children rarely take notes, but instead will remember most of what they heard. Most auditory learners tend to repeat things aloud, as the repetition helps them remember. These children do best with audio books, lectures and seminars and when others read instruction manuals to them.

Visual learners learn new skills by seeing the material presented. Visual learners enjoy coding and instruction manuals, and taking apart electronics and engines to see how they work. Using diagrams and other visual methods of learning are recommended for these types of learners.

Most people respond to a combination of these learning types and fall into several categories. What works for one subject or learning goal may not work for another. For instance, when Patrick was younger he was very much a tactile learner for math; wanting to use manipulatives and be in motion while completing his work. At the same time, he was also a visual learner; lattice math worked well where he could see how the problem was solved, and manipulatives were especially helpful for him to see how math happened. For long division, we made graphs and charts for him.

Often times when families tell me that their curriculum is not working out, it's the first question I ask. "What type of learner is your child?" Sometimes changing up your teaching style, rather than the curriculum itself, is enough to create a successful outcome.

Instead of doing the pages of worksheets that come with a text, try using the math manipulatives, or a dry erase board to solve the problems. Don't feel any assignment has to be completed in the way it's presented. In most instances, workbooks and written work only make a parent feel better that learning has occurred. Instead of writing a book report, try a re-enactment of a speech, or theater production. Instead of a written science experiment, have the child do the experiment in front of a live audience and poll results on what the outcome will be. Children change as fast as the weather and what works one day may not work the next. Learn to go with the flow and don't be afraid to try something new when what you've previously done is no longer working.

Methods of homeschooling is another area I don't spend a lot of time on when I meet with new homeschoolers. Homeschoolers rarely subscribe to one homeschooling method. Charlotte Mason, unit studies, school at home, classical education, unschooling, Waldorf, Montessori, and eclectic homeschooling are all choices to research. Spend some time to familiarize yourself with these methods, but don't settle on any one method too soon or even one method at all. Learn about each of these and feel free to pull out what parts work for you and your family. Do what resonates and what speaks to you. It is perfectly fine to use some of these methods, or a combination of all of them, or none at all.

Some families use different methods for different subjects. In our homeschool, we started with a Waldorf-ish curriculum for most subjects, but switched to a different math program when we found our chosen curriculum a bit too slow for our liking.

Some of the methods of homeschooling to research include:

School at home most resembles what is familiar to us as public school. While it may be done at home — curriculum, courses, subjects and even the schedule for the day most resemble that of the public school. Standardized testing is also usually implemented in some form as well.

Charlotte Mason was an early twentieth century British educator. She believed children learned best by using living books. Books that brought subject matter to life with hands on experience through lessons in the basic subjects of math, reading and writing. The Charlotte Mason method also takes the child's development and ability into consideration.

Out of the Box Learning

Unit studies are popular among homeschoolers and cover all the subject areas, while following a theme or interest area. For instance, a unit study on trains might cover the history of the transcontinental railway, math might include word problems about distance and speed or fuel consumption, science and the study of trains might consist of learning about the mechanics of the train engine, and English might be writing a paper about trains. While that is a simplistic unit study, they can be as complex or simple as you like, and easily adjusted for various learning or grade levels.

Unschooling is also a popular method of homeschooling. It is sometimes called interest-led learning or child-led learning. The news and media have often portrayed this method as letting the child do whatever they want or a complete hands-off approach to parenting, but that is not correct. Parents help facilitate the interest of the child by involving them in all kinds of activities from volunteering, to apprenticeships, to starting their own businesses. Unschoolers learn from everyday life experiences, and may not use school schedules or formal lessons unless the child shows interest. In the same way that children learn to walk and talk, unschooled children do learn their math, science, reading, and history; that is through a natural process of exploration.

The benefit to this lifestyle, is that unschooled children have the time to become authorities in areas of interest. The disadvantage may be that unschoolers do not follow the typical school subjects, and they may not do as well on grade-level assessments, or may have a harder time if they reenter the school system. The truth is all homeschoolers usually follow their own path and might not necessarily identify with specific grade levels. Because homeschoolers may not be studying the same subjects as those in public school, reentering an institutional setting may be difficult for some. In my experience, this isn't usually an issue and kids acclimate fairly quickly to what is expected of them academically. Where some homeschoolers have difficulty, is the formal schedule, lengthy hours of homework and long day in a public school setting. Kids are very resilient in almost every setting and readily meet both the academic requirements and expectations of public school should they return.

The Waldorf Method of homeschooling, based on the work of Rudolf Steiner, stresses the importance of educating the whole child through body, mind, and spirit. In the early grades, there is an emphasis on arts and crafts, music and movement, and nature. Children are taught to develop self-awareness and reasoning. Children in a Waldorf homeschool use a wide variety of classic literature and stories, and they create their own books as well. The Waldorf method discourages the use of technology because the belief is that it obstructs a child's creative nature.

The Montessori Method, named after educator Maria Montessori, is also popular in some homeschools. The Montessori Method stresses "no error learning," where the children learn at their own pace. Dr. Montessori designed her materials so that the child receives instant feedback on his progress through self-correcting materials. The Montessori homeschool avoids clutter and disarray. Wooden toys and manipulatives are preferred over plastic, and technology is discouraged.

Eclectic Homeschooling is often described as a varied blend of many of the methods mentioned above and more. Eclectic homeschoolers use everything in their environment to learn. That may mean textbooks, libraries, employing different methods, and different styles. The great joy with eclectic homeschooling is that it is customized to the individual needs of the child and no learning style is off limits.

Virtual schools may fall into the category of school at home. Some states require virtual school participation or offer that option to homeschoolers. Virtual schools are sometimes called *umbrella* schools, although not always. Originally used as a method of homeschooling for those in remote places, virtual schools are sometimes mandated to be under the purview of public schools so that grade reporting and grade level attainment can be monitored. Virtual

Out of the Box Learning

schools also don't require families to bring their text books with them as they travel.

Online or virtual schools will sometimes use language like "certified" or "credentialed," but they have little meaning for homeschoolers if this is not a requirement in your state. Since graduation requirements vary greatly by state, homeschoolers should check the credentials of the online school, or if a credentialed program is even needed in their state.

Public schools that utilize umbrella schools, get to keep students on the roster as an enrolled student, and are also able to keep both state and federal funding in some instances. Virtual schools do not have to pay for building costs or teachers' salaries, and may have large costs associated with them. They usually have long school hours — similar to the public school format, as well as deadlines for children's work to be submitted.

Families who are traveling or who move frequently, like military families, sometimes find virtual schools a better match for learning needs while traveling. Many homeschoolers find the use of umbrella or virtual schools too restrictive with the required logged hours, deadlines for work and lack of parent involvement. These are some of the very reasons parents choose not to replicate school at home however, this format might work well for the child who needs a highly structured routine, or who does not deal well with change.

I have seen all methods of homeschooling succeed, and I have seen them fail. Again, it's less about the method, and more about the parental involvement that determines a successful outcome. Combine whatever methods work for you and create your own individualized homeschool package for each child.

The Ideal Homeschool

We all want the ideal homeschool and educational path for our children, and it's easy to look at more seasoned homeschoolers and think how much they have their act together. Be gentle with yourself as you find your way. Seasoned homeschoolers didn't always have it all together but what they have learned is family, money management, research skills, time management, and organizational skills that would rival a CEO of any business.

Homeschooling parents are master budgeters, multitaskers, risk takers, research analysts, and are leaders in meeting deadlines. Until you have seen a homeschooling mom with seven kids manage a monthly food and mortgage budget, juggle those seven kids' sports schedule; teach them, feed them, do laundry, volunteer at the soup kitchen and still keep her marriage together, you haven't seen anything. And none of it is ideal or perfect.

The ideal homeschool doesn't exist so don't try to create one. The only bar we should try to live up to is the one we create for our own family. If you are a Type-A or an academically oriented person, guess what your

Out of the Box Learning

homeschool will look like? If you are a care-free parent with few rules, guess what your homeschool will like? If you try to create a life or homeschool based on the needs of another family, you will likely not be successful. When the days seem tough, reflect on what is important and why you chose to homeschool in the first place. Regroup with other homeschooling moms when your picture of ideal falls to pieces.

New homeschoolers sometimes start their homeschooling experience by mimicking public school. Inevitably, there will be a subject you struggle with, and you will likely teach your kids this subject in a less than stellar way. We all have those shortcomings. I certainly did and still do. When my daughter was studying chemistry, I had to switch textbooks three times for it to make sense for her and for me. I hadn't looked at chemistry since I was in college, and brushing off those cobwebs in my brain was sure harder than I thought it would be. The subject had changed so much through the years that I was stuck, and she was frustrated.

Thankfully, I found a teacher's manual that helped me and a text that was much simpler to understand. This is also a great time to utilize those ____ for Dummies, books. They are great as a refresher course for terminology, and to remind you of things within the subject that you may have long forgotten. Had I not been able to decipher this subject, I had some friends I could have called on for help. Make sure you are calling for help when you need it. Other homeschooling parents, consultants, the internet, and people in your community can all help. You do not need to be your child's only teacher, or to feel like a subject is beyond your knowledge.

If the overwhelming task of trying to do it all is wearing you thin — streamline what you are doing. Do your children really need to attend dance class three times per week? Maybe once a week is enough. Do you really need to go to every birthday party and family celebration? Do you really need to sign up for every field trip and class that is offered? Do they need another academic class just because it is the expected path? Does it matter if your sink is full of dishes for the fourth day in a row? Bow out, pare down, and simplify as much as you can. If you are stuck, recognize that and ask for help.

• • •

Homeschooling Through Illness

A significant portion of my homeschooling days has been spent dealing with illness either of my children or myself. Illness, whether acute or chronic, will strike your homeschool at some point and you will have to come up with Plan B. I know several homeschooled children and parents with chronic illness or life threatening allergies, that make homeschooling work for them. These kids would miss far too much public school due to the illness, or worse, be exposed to things that could potentially harm or even kill them.

In our state, if a child is on home confinement, (due to illness, medical or other issues) but still enrolled in the public school, the district is only required to provide five hours of tutoring time each week. Homeschooled kids, even while ill, can usually complete far more work than these few hours that are provided by public school.

Even if a child is bedridden, they might be able to read and complete much more work than their public school peers. Homeschooled children do not fall behind like their public school counterparts because their learning begins where they left off, not according to what a premade lesson plan tells them where they should be. There really isn't a "behind." There is also no guilt if a parent has an illness and needs to put a child back in public school. It's also perfectly okay if you keep them home. Family is so important and when days are short, do what you can to make the best of the time together.

In 2008, I was diagnosed with Lyme disease. I spent the first two years seeking a diagnosis while undergoing doctor appointment after doctor appointment, with an endless calendar of medical testing. By the second year, I was incredibly ill and thought I was dying. The disease had a profound effect on what I was able to do, and I spent much time in bed due to intense fatigue, headaches and pain. I had trouble reading more than a paragraph due to the Lyme and co-infections being in my brain, and I could not walk more than a few steps without needing to sit down, as my legs refused to carry me. My headaches lasted six months and double vision was frequent. My mood swings were horrible, and pain in my joints and muscles was constant. When a diagnosis was finally made, I spent ten months on intravenous antibiotic therapy at home, several weeks in the hospital from complications from Lyme and became very debilitated.

Continuing my nursing career became impossible and after multiple leaves of absence, I finally left my job of twenty years. The final straw came when I almost overdosed a patient. While I caught the error before the medication even made it to the patient's bedside, it was a huge wakeup call for me. All of the things I loved doing, had become impossible.

I was still homeschooling my three children when I was sick and it was an incredible struggle. We never considered sending them back to public school because honestly, if I hadn't had my family surrounding me or there to help me when I was my sickest, I don't know how I would have made it through that terrible time.

During my sickest moments and while I was hospitalized, my kids' education plan had to be altered. My husband did some math in the evenings with the kids, while my days were spent on my bed or on the couch, as the kids read stories to me and we talked about their work. Correcting work was an impossible nightmare for me, never mind teaching them anything new. Using the teacher's manuals and instruction guides really got me through rough patches in helping my kids, and Larry did most of the correcting of their work.

Thankfully we had a complete curriculum package during my illness that included lesson plans. Not having to plan lessons was a huge relief and lifted both the guilt and burden of homeschooling my kids, when I thought they weren't getting enough. On the days I did feel well enough to get out, we would go to the park and catch frogs, and take an easier approach to learning. The kids helped with dinner preparations and cleaning but really what they learned from that whole experience is the importance of caring for family.

Despite being so sick, I cherish the times on the couch, snuggled under a blanket when the kids could see how hard their mother was fighting to get well. Looking back, we watched the history channel and did spelling on the computer because it had auto correct, and we got creative with crafts, and relatives and friends took the kids on day trips. We learned about science by watching videos on the internet, and picked places on the map to learn about geography. There was still lots of learning going on when we sat back to look at all we did. What I learned from the experience was that my kids were fully equipped to learn with or without my help.

Time being ill is like any other obstacle that comes up in life, and you will need to make adjustments in your homeschooling, should life changes happen. Consider any obstacle a chance for you to get creative, to see what new ideas pop up, what you might let go of and, where you might make some changes in homeschooling that are no longer working.

Seek out help when you need it, scale things back when it gets complicated and know the few missed days, weeks, or sometimes even a year, won't really matter in the long haul because your children will still be learning. Illness does not need to halt homeschooling. Just as kids learn at different paces, homeschooling can usually fit into family situations when illness or other things become a struggle.

Getting Through the Hard Days

Homeschooling will hopefully bring you great joy, but there are also days that it is incredibly hard. Remember that there are hard days for public and private school teachers too, and just because we homeschool, doesn't guarantee that it will be a smooth ride. Let go of the illusion that homeschooling will be all rainbows and ponies. It just doesn't happen that way.

In my coaching work parents rarely come in joyous; they come seeking help because they don't know where to start, or something is not going well in their homeschool. The hard days of homeschooling are rarely talked about, until a parent emails, or posts to social media that they are giving up, or are throwing their hands up in despair and don't know what to do.

A life crisis, goals or homeschooling expectations have not been met, and the parents are confused and discouraged as to what could have gone wrong and how to remedy the situation. These parents have read every book and researched everything they could find out about homeschooling and yet, it still isn't working. Why? Because even the most experienced homeschoolers need support at some time on their journey. This is a normal part of the homeschooling process.

Beverly Burgess

A mom recently contacted me and told me that she had a month where sibling rivalry was at an all-time high, there was little actual school work happening and the fighting amongst the kids in the house had exploded. She was ready to give up, incredibly tired and felt like a failure. There are days when your children will be like oil and water; when a sideways glance or someone being in their space, is enough to set off a family war. There will be poking and name calling, and instigating and rebellion, and not-so-proud parenting moments.

Let me share a story with you of one of my not so proud parenting moments I had while homeschooling. When my youngest son was eight years old, he flat out refused to do any work for weeks. The work he did manage to complete showed a very poor effort, and was only attempted in the most lackadaisical way, so that he could say he finished the assignment. His attitude was poor, and he was refusing to do chores and other things asked of him. We talked about how every child needs an education and how it was mandatory by law, and how all people in the family need to contribute to the good of the family. He sat there with his arms folded and still refused to do anything or listen to anything I said, and his short answer quips and snarky attitude pushed all my parenting buttons.

My anger grew and I felt disrespected, disappointed and could not understand how a child that I raised, had such a poor work ethic and nasty disposition. So I loaded him in the car and drove him down to the local police station. I yelled at him during the entire car ride about his attitude, lack of respect, and how he or I might possibly spend time in jail because he refused to do school work and was now truant.

He sat stoically in the back seat of the car the whole way there, like he wasn't going to give me an inch in my parenting. Once we pulled into the police station, he burst into tears and started sobbing and hyperventilating, while trying to apologize. My heart sank and I felt like my gut had been eviscerated. I turned my head away and wiped away my own tears as I slowly drove back down the road.

Out of the Box Learning

I felt like a terrible parent and a failure, and knew that my own patience and understanding weren't anywhere to be found that day.

We made it through that terrible moment and the next day too; a root beer float and a couple of chocolate chip cookies calmed us both down during our long talk. But as a parent, I felt defeated, guilty and unhappy with what I put my son through. I did apologize to him, and we talked about how mommies and daddies have hard days just like kids, and how we would all try to do better. Kids are forgiving and resilient and my son moved on from that awful day rather quickly. For me, it was a moment I won't ever forget. It's really important that you remember that you will have really proud moments, and then moments when you think you can't possibly go on with parenting or with homeschooling, and you will feel like the worst parent ever.

Parents need to determine if the problems they are experiencing really have to do with homeschooling, or if they are just everyday life and parenting issues. Most are quick to blame homeschooling, but look deeply at the root cause of what is triggering your distress and give it good thought before making any decisions on whether to continue to homeschool or not. More than likely, it is just a season of parenting and will quickly pass.

Homeschooling While Working

Many parents that I consult with would like to homeschool, but are concerned because one or more parents works part or full time. They wonder how they can juggle and manage it all, and come seeking advice and reassurance. I was a homeschooling and working mother for over eight years. My nursing career allowed me to work second shift, so I only had to find a babysitter for a few hours in the afternoon until my husband came home from work. As my family grew, I reduced my time at work further, and started working per diem. Then, I switched to the night shift on weekends when my husband was home.

While many are not able to change their work schedules so easily, know that homeschooling while working is not impossible. The great freedom of homeschooling is that we don't have to schedule learning from 9 a.m. to 3 p.m. every day. You can homeschool in the afternoon, in the evening, and on weekends, and one parent or both can be responsible for sharing in their children's learning.

Parents often tell me that they can't afford for one parent to stay home. In 2010 when I was abruptly out of work due to illness, we lost my income. While I had applied for assistance, it would be

Out of the Box Learning

another two years before it was approved, and we had to totally re-evaluate our spending and budget. Disability income was also only about one-third of what my monthly salary was, and as a family we needed to completely restructure our spending habits and figure out wants versus needs.

Often times I hear, "It must be nice to stay at home, that's a luxury that I can't afford!" Most homeschoolers do not lead glamourous lifestyles, but we have all we need. If you find your work fulfilling, then by all means continue to do so. But if you find yourself questioning if you can work and homeschool, reduce your hours, or even give up one salary; the answer is likely yes. What is surprising to families is how much they actually save when a parent stops working. No longer are you paying for daycare, lunches, work clothes, gas, parking and daily coffee. Sometimes it's a huge eye opener to families when they realize one partner's entire salary was going toward daycare expenses, parking fees and wardrobes for work. Take a really hard look at what you spend your money on before saying you cannot afford to homeschool. If you need budgeting help to make it work, reach out to another homeschooling parent. Many parents who run their own businesses seamlessly meld their work time and homeschool time. The flexibility in scheduling suits them well.

My family manages on a strict budget and everything must be accounted for including home repairs, birthdays, homeschool curriculum and date nights. While we don't get to take extended vacations, we do manage to get out and enjoy ourselves. One-parent working households are a decision like everything else. You have to decide where your priorities are, what your goals are, and where your money will go. If you take a detailed look at your finances, you might see that the $5 you spend on mocha lattes every morning will buy a pretty decent curriculum package at the end of the year, or will pay for your groceries for a few weeks if you save that money instead of spending it. We got rid of our landline and instead, only have our cell phones. We reduced our cable TV to a basic package since we don't watch much TV anyway. We forgo new cars and instead use our cars until the repairs cost more than the value of the car, or until the car dies. Then we buy the best used car our budget will allow. We switched to monthly food shopping, buy in bulk, and have saved money by not running to the grocery store every week for supplies or extras.

During the summer we grow our own vegetables and I preserve whatever harvest I gather. We grow fruit trees and berries and make jam. I have a bread machine and make my own bread. We are frugal with clothes shopping and gift giving. Certainly, you don't have to be a homesteading family to homeschool; but if you aren't good at gardening or don't like to garden, then swap some produce for a knit blanket or tax filing help. The point is to find your skills, share them, and make a few extra dollars or barter wherever you can. If you need to keep the second salary in the family, look at freelance work that you can do from home to supplement your income. I grew up in a family of eight kids so my mother taught me how to extend meals that would last for several days. I enjoy gardening so being able to grow my own food when I can, is a joy for me. Watching your pennies does not mean that you have to eat beans and pasta every night. There are hundreds of ways to make it work!

If homeschooling on one income, or even when both parents are working, is a concern, I encourage you to give good scrutiny to your budget. What do you not need to pay for anymore or aren't using? What would you give up for your kids' education? You might be surprised at how much you can save, and what you are able to make instead of buy. Trimming your budget is not that hard, and asking other homeschool moms how they manage their spending is a great way to learn more.

Organizing Your Homeschool Space

I wrote earlier that the only two things you needed to homeschool were love and self-care. While that's true, organizational skills while homeschooling are a great asset to have. Being able to find and keep track of all the things needed for homeschooling, will save you a lot of headaches in the long run. I have found that keeping three-ring-binders for important documents that you might need, a helpful tool. Have the kids keep binders of their work as well, and try to keep textbooks and supplies in one spot so things don't get lost.

One of the biggest investments we make in our home is our computers and upgrades. There is nothing more frustrating than trying to access our online lesson planner and having our computer decide that the bright shiny new software is not compatible with our old, outdated computer. My kids do most of their work on the computer and having good working equipment is essential to our homeschool, and for staying connected with the world.

Parents today need to be computer savvy as much as kids. Registering for homeschooling events, connecting on social media, doing research and homeschool work are all things we use our computer for. Parents have asked me if homeschoolers need computers.

Yes, they do. We live in a technological age where children and adults are connected to the wider world through the internet. We cannot be afraid of the perceived dangers of technology, and instead need to put safeguards in place while our children are using what they need to make their homeschooling experience successful.

Homeschooling parents will need to use the computer as well to keep track of lessons, saved websites and to search for other things to include in lesson plans. If you aren't able to have your own computer in your home, you should consider using the library. Most libraries have multiple computers for patrons' general use. While I like a basic spiral notebook for my own notes and lists, I would be lost as would my children, without technology.

The first year you homeschool, you will buy everything you think you will need to homeschool, and will not use most of it. Much of what you buy will be necessary for a public school classroom, but very little of it is needed for a homeschool. Our very first year of homeschooling, I shopped at every back-to-school sale and bought pencil boxes, cute notebooks, posters, and every art supply I could find. I still shop back to school sales, but have pared my list down considerably. I also recommend buying supplies for your own desk and use, and not allowing the kids to use them. Pencils, dry erase markers, pens, tape and the like will quickly disappear from your desk if you give the kids free use. Better to replenish the needed items for the kids and teach them to take care of these materials, than to give up your own. Be sure to teach the kids about putting caps on markers and returning items to bins. It will save you time and money when kids learn good care of items, and learn to clean up at the end of the day.

I am fortunate to have a designated homeschool space, but it's not necessary. You will accumulate a LOT of homeschooling materials such as texts, art projects, science experiments and lab equipment. For our family it was easiest to contain most everything to one room. We have a large table set up so everyone can work and sit together. I recommend making the space as un-school like as possible. If it makes more sense to keep supplies in a kitchen pantry, then do that. Make it work for you because this is your home, not a school or classroom.

When my family first decided to homeschool, I unfortunately had to share my personal office space with our homeschooling space. I don't recommend this. I made it work, but the kid's stuff often spills onto my work space, and unfinished projects litter the table. Some days, I have to stop everything and clean off the clutter and reorganize. It gives the kids a chance to purge scrap paper and get rid of work they no longer need. Both kids mostly prefer to use other rooms in the house to do homeschool work though. My teen prefers the couch in the living room, my middle schooler prefers his bed, and the kitchen table is a favorite place too because the kids can snack and do work at the same time.

At the end of the day, everything gets put back into the homeschool room so we can find it the next day. Clutter makes me feel out of control, so having everything contained in one space just makes things easier to find. If you don't have a designated space, try to choose one bookshelf or one cabinet in the living room to contain the mess and supplies. Teach the kids from the first day to return homeschool items to their designated place, it will help keep the clutter and mess to a minimum.

I have somewhat divided our homeschool room into the kids' space and my "teacher" space. The kids have a large, vertical bookshelf with a designated shelf for each of them to keep texts, notebooks, pencil boxes etc. The other shelves are used for math manipulatives, scrap paper, and frequently used items like reference books. The microscope and globe and other infrequently used items are stored on the top of the book shelf, still within easy reach but out of the way. We have a five drawer plastic storage center for extra paper, glue, binders, tape, colored paper, rulers and science equipment like lab slides. The closet in the room holds art supplies, and office supplies like reams of paper and extra binders. Crock pots or large jars are on the center of the table and contain markers, scissors, pencils and pens. We purchased a $3.00 plastic cleaning carrel and use it to store colored pencils, protractors, erasers and anything else the kids would need on a frequent basis. Carrels make it easy to transport art supplies and keep everything neat. Many items, like large paper cutters, can be purchased once to keep on hand through all of your homeschooling years. My kids are older so I don't need crayons anymore, but we do need much more printer paper.

Homeschooling supplies need not cost a lot, and there are some staples that you will likely need. Determine what you need in your own homeschool according to what your family uses and the ages of your children.

Each year I buy:
- 2 boxes of printer paper (sometimes more).
- Ink cartridges-amount varies.
- 4 boxes of #2 Ticonderoga pencils.
- 4 boxes of pens.
- 2 packages of pink erasers.
- 25 single subject spiral notebooks. (These get placed in binders and last longer and are neater than loose leaf paper).
- 4 three ring binders (2 for each child).
- 2 boxes of colored pencils.
- 2 packages each of small and large notecards.
- 10 rolls scotch tape/4 rolls masking tape/4 rolls duct tape.

Supplies to have on hand (depending on age and stage of child):
- Printer.
- Large paper cutter.
- Binder clips/paper clips.

Out of the Box Learning

- Pushpins/tacks.
- Paint/Crayons (may need to buy yearly or more often for younger ages).
- Three-hole punch/paper punches.
- Glue sticks (may be a yearly or twice yearly purchase).
- Kid/adult scissors.
- Computer or laptop.
- Storage containers in various sizes (these hold everything from unfinished art projects to math manipulatives to Legos).

At the middle and highschool level, the expectation should be that most work is completed on the computer. Kids absolutely need computer skills for homeschool work and in the general world, and it is required in college, so start them early. My middle schooler does his writing assignments on the computer, but most all other work in workbooks and notebooks. The highschooler uses the computer exclusively for her work except for her math workbook and for notetaking.

The homeschool room still functions as my office too, and I have my own large bookshelf that holds teacher's manuals, my computer and software guide books, reference books for homeschooling and all of my coaching business information. I have a two drawer lateral file to the right of my desk that holds homeschooling information and personal files. We also invested money in a quality office printer that can fax, scan and copy. You will be doing a lot of printing and copying as homeschoolers, so it's worth the investment in a decent printer.

We have a dry erase board and small cork board on the wall. The kids like using the dry erase board for math problems and equations. The dry erase board is a great teaching tool, for showing new math concepts, to leave notes for the kids, or to put reminders up about what events are coming up. It is the most used tool in our homeschool next to the computers.

A good scheduling device is vital to keeping your sanity in homeschooling. We use Google calendar as well as a master, dry erase calendar for our household management. With one child in college, two other children, sports, volunteering, and work schedules; a master calendar becomes critical to keeping it all under control. All of my kids have been taught to put their own events on the virtual calendar including sports schedules, babysitting, classes and job interviews. After so many years of homeschooling they know if it doesn't make it on the calendar, they might not make it to the event because someone else's event was scheduled in its place.

Goals in the homeschool setting are just as important as they are in other areas of life. Most homeschoolers often aren't sure what goals they might have for their children as they begin this journey. It's one of the first questions I ask when I meet with new homeschoolers. "What do you want for your children?" I encourage family-centered goals to start with since homeschooling is such an extension of your family. Maybe your goal is family dinners at least three times a week, or family game night once a month. While you might question what this has to do with homeschooling, it really is the start for a smoother family lifestyle and stronger family ties. Once that occurs, homeschooling comes much more easily. Build the bonds first, then worry about the homeschooling goals.

When it comes to homeschooling, keep goals loose and flexible. Is the main goal to help them enjoy learning again, or is your goal more specific like to increase reading fluency? Is one of your goals to teach them independence, or to be exposed to a wider variety of opportunities? Rather than make very specific goals, like "finish math textbook" — keep it changeable like "gain confidence in math skills." Start with smaller goals, feel free to change them as your homeschool and family life changes, and be sure you are not basing your goals off of completing a curriculum.

Out of the Box Learning

I have a master binder that I keep next to my computer, and it has everything I need right at my fingertips to help me keep my homeschool organized. I use a three-ring binder and section divider tabs. There is a master area in the front that I use for notes for things like writing down a curriculum I want to explore, or making a doctor's appointment.

My master binder includes:
- Monthly & Yearly Calendar/attendance.
- Password sheet for online curriculum or planners.
- Any notices from school department related to homeschooling.
- Listing of current curriculum being used for each child.
- Scope and Sequence for each child.
- The EZ Grader (ezgrader.com).
- Website url's of any sites I frequent often.
- Receipts from any homeschool curriculum purchases through the year.
- Quick Reference Sheets:
  -Math cheat sheet — because who can ever remember measurement conversions?
  -Periodic Table & elements list.
  -United States & Capitals list.
  -US Presidents list.
  -Writing Rubrics.
  Children's Section-
- Saved work (1-2 worksheets or other "proof" of learning per subject, per child).
- Child safe information (fingerprints and current photo).
- Monthly & Yearly curriculum outline.
- Immunization, health records & birth certificate documents. (needed for sports teams and camps).

If your state requires you to keep a portfolio of your homeschooling, I suggest keeping one or two papers from each child per subject per month. Choose papers that show improvement, or that shows how a child began learning and one paper that shows the mastery of the skill. Mastery of subjects does not need to be shown only in worksheets. Photographs of classes, field trips and any homeschooling experiences is a great way to document all you have accomplished. At the end of each year, I file everything into a manila folder, label the front, and place it with the other homeschool records on a basement shelf. I keep completed school work for three years only and then toss them in the garbage.

Highschool documents should be kept until the child graduates or goes to college as you will need to provide transcripts or portfolios to the college depending on what major is chosen.

Curriculum Searching

What do we use for curriculum? Parents may have just decided to homeschool but it's the first question that they ask on this new journey. New homeschoolers have likely spent many years in public school, and are used to someone else choosing a curriculum for their child. They may have never even explored school textbooks other than their own children's books, or given curriculum a second thought. Now faced with the daunting task of choosing the very thing that seems most important to their child's education; it's easy to feel lost and unsure.

A huge eye opener for me was when I realized that my choice of curriculum really didn't matter much at all. For most, this seems counter to what was learned in public school — that the curriculum is the central necessity to learning. I'm going to repeat what I said in the beginning chapters. Kids are inherent learners and any curriculum, whether cheaply priced or expensive, or no curriculum at all, will likely serve you and your children just fine. Anything chosen should still be a match for your child's learning style but beyond that criteria— not much else matters. Shocking, right? Textbooks and teacher's manuals help the parents more than they help the children, because they help us with knowing what comes next.

Teacher's manuals are important to homeschooling parents because they help us relearn what may have been forgotten, and help us to push away those cobwebs of long forgotten material. They have been hugely helpful in teaching my own kids.

Children don't know the difference between a cheap or expensive curriculum, or a mom who created her own unit studies, or just printed off a worksheet from a website. I have seen fabulous unit studies created by kids and by homeschooling parents. Many of these kids and parents have been homeschooling for many years, and know what homeschoolers need. Information found in textbooks is just as easily found on the internet, and a few quick clicks will lead you to most anything you need for your children's studies.

As homeschoolers we are not limited to just textbooks. Field trips for history, sports teams, online classes, travel, and a host of other activities, all help to round out our learning without the use of textbooks. Learning in the homeschool setting is genuine, because nothing is designed in an attempt to produce a standard result, or to meet standards set by other persons. We want the best educational outcome for our children, but a curriculum does not equal learning, nor does it guarantee educational success.

So why bother with textbooks at all in the homeschool setting? Textbooks can help guide parents when they are at a loss in what to teach. They can be more of a guide in subject matter, rather than a manuscript to follow. When it comes to choosing homeschool curriculum the choices are vast, so begin with researching what your state homeschooling laws are and what subjects you must teach, if any. While homeschoolers tend not to compartmentalize learning into subjects, some states do require reporting in this method. Most states require the basic courses of language arts, math, history, science, and physical education. They may also define what specifically is taught at each grade level. Be sure you know what is required in your state before you begin.

Secondly, decide if you want a religious or secular based curriculum. You don't have to choose only one or the other, and in

Out of the Box Learning

fact many homeschoolers choose both. Just be aware at the high-school level, that some colleges may not accept creation science courses that are listed on transcripts. You will need to research this further if your child is heading toward higher education.

I have a hard time letting go of books of any sort and I'm an admitted curriculum hoarder. Now that I am in my eleventh year of homeschooling, I have finally been able to purge a good amount of texts. Some I sold, some were gifted to other homeschoolers, but most were given to our homeschool group's resource library for others to enjoy. I have come to a point where I know which curriculum works for our family and which ones don't. As my youngest child ages up through the grades, it has become easier to let go of curriculum for grades that he has completed. This was a harder task when my kids were at various grade levels, or different ages and stages in homeschooling.

I love browsing curriculum. I spend a lot time reviewing and going through curriculum, not only for my own benefit, but so that I can counsel other homeschoolers on things that might be a match for their learning. My teacher's manuals and all my texts are marked up, the margins are penciled with notes, and they are highlighted and have tagged page corners too.

I have lost some resale value on used curriculum because of my penchant for putting my thoughts inside the books, but this method works well for me. When purchasing used homeschool curriculum, I actually look for previous markings from other homeschool parents. You would be surprised the insight previous owners might have on chapter books, how they often refer to other literature or resources.

During our first year of homeschooling, we used a boxed curriculum that was priced on the higher side. I found it very worth its value and it suited our needs well. The lesson plans along with all the texts, workbooks and other material were all provided, so it was a matter of just opening the lesson plan to see what needed to be completed for the day and checking off the completed work. The boxed curriculum got me through some difficult days when I was ill. We used it for several years until I figured out what homeschooling looked like for us. Be aware though, that many complete curriculums may be standardized and include a lot of busy work that isn't necessary in the homeschool setting. Read through the day's lessons and eliminate anything that isn't needed. If you decide that a boxed curriculum is right for you, know that you can supplement any area that doesn't suit your needs or needs more exploration, with an alternate curriculum, project or unit study.

Parents can do an internet search for "scope and sequence" for whatever grade they need. A scope and sequence summarizes what is customarily taught, and the sequence in which it will be taught at various grade levels. While not a curriculum, it will give parents ideas on what topics to cover when imagination and ideas run thin. As homeschoolers we are not limited to a grade level, so if your child's expected scope and sequence grade isn't providing what you need, search another grade level and find something that is. Don't be afraid to go out of order on what the scope and sequence suggests is the proper timeline. Sometimes looking a grade level or two ahead can provide great resources in some new subject matter for your children.

Some parents choose to use the public school curriculum because they are comforted in knowing that they will be keeping up with peers of the same age and grade. In general, public school curriculum is limiting and doesn't take advantage of the flexibility of homeschooling, or the many opportunities available to homeschoolers. Common Core State Standards also do not suit many homeschoolers needs, as we tend to reach milestones and goals at different times and with far different outcomes than public schooled children. If you have left public school because of common core or the district's curriculum, consider why you would want to use these again in your homeschool.

Depending on what your homeschool state laws demand of you, you might have to submit an education plan to your district. Education plans may include the texts being used, subjects and courses that are taught, and expected grade levels. Check with your local homeschool group to see what is needed. Unschoolers, who

Out of the Box Learning

may not always define their learning by courses, texts or subjects, can get creative when submitting educational plans. Karate classes will meet physical education requirements, Shakespeare Theater classes may cover British Literature, extracurriculars or even an English requirement. Math or Geometry can be incorporated into a woodworking class, and world studies or foreign language can be done through travel or immersion programs. One family in our group even learned Italian from the exchange student they were hosting. The idea is to think out of the box when designing learning opportunities for your homeschooled children.

If your state or homeschooling group offers a yearly conference or used curriculum sale, you can browse the curriculum before buying and ask lots of questions. It's also a great opportunity to bring your children and have them choose curriculum. That's right, your children should be as actively involved in choosing the curriculum as you are, and it must be a fit for both parent and child. If homeschooling results in tears for the child or the parent, it's time to reevaluate the curriculum, or the method. The only acceptable tears in homeschooling are tears of joy!

Early in my own homeschooling journey I purchased a fancy language arts curriculum. It was filled with glossy, beautiful workbook style pages and real photographs instead of clip art. It was colorful, recommended by a top publisher, and was used by many public schools. I paid a lot of money for it and thought it was stunning. It resembled what I thought learning should look like, at least in public school. However, my youngest child hated it and would cry every time it was language arts time. While the book seemed to fit all the needs of a comprehensive language arts program, my son was overwhelmed by the busyness and colors of the artwork, repetitiveness of the lessons, and the many examples that needed to be completed in each exercise.

The photos were misleading and made it difficult to determine what answer was expected. A photo of a frog was not meant to be a frog but of "hop." The flag picture was "fly" and rabbit was "hare." He got so many wrong in the workbook, and it required so much correction and deciphering, that even I wasn't sure of what they were asking. After about a week of torturing my youngest with this, we swapped it out for a very simple black and white, recycled paper version with fewer examples needing completion. The simple outline had a much less overwhelming structure and provided him with exactly what he needed. Each text essentially had the same information, but only one was a match for my child. While I still prefer the pretty books, they have to work for both parent and child, and in this case, did not.

    Homeschooling websites and blogs have extensive curriculum reviews by homeschooling parents that are helpful in finding what you need. They will tell you whether it's worth the money, too complicated or much too easy, as well as what the customer service was like when they needed assistance. Homeschooling parents can direct you to online resources for finding textbooks and other homeschooling needs at rock bottom prices. Social media is also a huge help to homeschooling parents. If you find a curriculum that you think you are interested in, ask your homeschooling group parents what their thoughts are. Most parents are happy to meet with you to let you browse the curriculum, and chances are many will chime in and give you a full review. Don't be afraid to toss, sell or donate a curriculum that isn't working for you. What isn't working for you may work great for another homeschooling family.

    Local libraries are a terrific resource to homeschoolers and will often lend books to homeschoolers for extended periods of time. Our local library has a whole curriculum section available to both public school and homeschool teachers. Microscopes, slides, posters, lesson plans, and posters are just a few of the things available to us that we may borrow. Librarians will pull together books to create a whole unit study if you let them know what you are looking for. Call ahead or visit with your librarian to see if they will bundle some books together for a topic you may be studying. This is also a great way to utilize material for a cooperative program.

Out of the Box Learning

When choosing courses, homeschoolers see no difference in the importance of extracurricular activities, compared to core classes. Public schools see the arts and music as "outside" the standard English or Math core curriculum, and not necessarily essential or important to learning. Time allotted to these classes tends to be less than other core classes, if they are offered at all. More and more humanities and art classes are being cut from annual budgets, or the amount of time allowed in these programs is traded for more test preparations or class time on "real" subjects. This doesn't happen in the homeschool setting where children can fully explore all areas of interest without someone else deciding if they are important enough to study.

As you begin to review your curriculum, remember that no curriculum or method will be an absolute fit for your needs or family. Curriculum websites usually have sample pages of texts that you can review before purchasing, or the company will send you a catalog that will have more in-depth details to help you make a decision.

Curriculum costs can vary greatly. There are many free online curriculum resources as well as other curricula that can cost thousands of dollars per child. Decide what budget you have or want to spend per child. For our family, budgeting for school supplies is no different than planning for other household expenses. Do not make homeschool expenses a last minute decision; be sure to consider everything and price shop for cost comparisons.

If you are considering a large purchase from a well-known publisher, ask them when their annual sale is. If you tell them that you will need to wait until the sale to purchase, they will most always give you the discount early. Don't be afraid to ask them for the sale or promotional discount price too. Once they know you can purchase immediately, most will be happy to give the discount. Used texts in good condition have suited us just fine and comparing ISBN numbers and publication dates have assured that we have exactly what we need each year. Putting a shout out on homeschooling social media sites is another great way to acquire curriculum. An ISO (in search of) post will almost always yield what you need.

Beverly Burgess

Each year I create a spreadsheet of every book purchased, the approximate grade level, the ISBN numbers, the cost, and where I bought it. While this seems a bit over the top for some, it has saved me a huge amount of time, since I use the texts for other children in subsequent years. Homeschooling books get lost or misplaced, and workbooks are consumable and need to be reordered if used again. Keeping track of all of this as you acquire texts, will save time and effort in all your homeschooling years.

If a text is needed for a specific grade or syllabus, the replacement can easily be found or repurchased without much trouble if you have the ISBN number and publisher, or if you know the company where you purchased it from. I write the approximate grade level inside the cover of every book as soon as it arrives. I can't tell you how many times I thought a book was a certain grade level only to discover I was wrong. Most publishers do not put grade levels on their texts even for public school. This small step has been a lifesaver for me. Get in the habit of labeling your books as soon as they arrive, and you will have far less headaches as the years move on.

I also put stickers on the bindings of every text and color label them on a spreadsheet to match. For instance, tenth-grade books have a yellow horizontal sticker and are labeled "10". This corresponds to my master sheet, and when I'm storing the books for another year, makes them easy to find, and there is no question of what grade level it is. I store all of our texts by grade level so that I can find everything I need. You may choose to store them by subject, or even color if you choose. Consumable workbooks should be purchased new every year. In my experience, they get too much wear and tear to use again. Some parents save workbooks and make copies of the pages for other children in their homes to preserve the original. This works well for a couple of years but workbooks and paperbacks don't last long in general, and are best replaced after a few uses. Devise a system that works well for you and your home.

Homeschooling Multiple Grades & Ages

Public schools require that children, who are the same age but who don't necessarily have the same skills, be placed in the same classroom or grade. Additionally, they use curriculum designed only for that grade. Homeschooling allows children to be taught and to share curriculum across multiple grade, skill levels and by using a variety of curriculum that is not boxed in by grade.

Teaching children in multiple grades can be challenging. If you have a fourth and fifth grader, one curriculum may suffice, and tailoring it for those with more or less skills can work well. As the older children age, younger kids slide into the next grade position. By the time the oldest is in fifth grade, there may be three or four kids who are of school age, all with individual sets of curriculum, all costing large amounts of money, and not necessarily coordinated or organized in any way that works for you, the homeschool teacher. Kids are often at various levels in their learning and for those that excel or need more assistance, you can supplement with larger projects, or increase or decrease the difficulty of the work when necessary. Many homeschooling parents successfully use one curriculum for multiple grade levels, and tailor fit the work to the ages and stages of their children's developmental growth.

The secret to success in homeschooling is letting go of specific grade levels, at least in the early years. If you switch your focus to subjects or skill area and not grade level, homeschooling multiples will work more along the lines of the one room school house method. Kids will automatically perform at THEIR "grade level" or according to their skill set. This is an important piece of homeschooling — kids perform at their OWN level, rather than the expectation of a grade, or specific outcome of completion. Grade levels become irrelevant when choosing the next text or idea to follow in your child's learning path. The question to ask is, "What's the next thing my child needs, or wants to learn? What is the next skill to learn?"

Time management and multitasking is imperative when homeschooling multiple children. Toddlers and young children can be kept occupied with busy boxes, and older kids can be taught when babies are napping. Busy boxes filled and changed out regularly with manipulatives, play-doh, counting bears and other activities, help a young child to feel as if they have their own belongings when "school-time" starts. Let them make a mess if they are happy and occupied. Sometimes cleaning up play-doh crumbs is worth it for forty-five minutes of uninterrupted one-on-one time with another child. Most homeschoolers just tend to involve the toddlers in whatever activity is going on that day. Life doesn't really stop when you have young children and you might be surprised how easy it is to homeschool multiple children.

Those who homeschool with toddlers underfoot will be surprised to see how much the little ones absorb by watching and listening to the other children and family members. I have heard time and time again, that toddlers learned all their colors, or even learned to read because an older sibling enjoyed reading to the younger ones, or the young child just seemed to absorb his learning.

Out of the Box Learning

Middle and highschoolers can and should be mostly independent with work, allowing you time to work with younger children. Parents with children at this level should be more of a resource for their children, helping when new concepts are covered and prompting discussions. I started my kids with a daily assignment sheet as soon as they could read. When the work was completed, they checked it off and gave it back to me. As they progress through the years or grades, assignments became more in depth but the same method of checking off work when completed, still works well for us today.

Be sure that whatever time you do give each child is uninterrupted. Explaining a new concept or reviewing one that needs more attention, is not a time to return phone calls or browse social media. Be present for your children while you are homeschooling them and give them your undivided attention.

Planning the Full Year

After I have chosen my curriculum for the coming homeschool year, I wait patiently for the big curriculum box to arrive, or begin my yearly planning by pulling out curriculum we already have. I spend more time in this area than anywhere else because, the hours spent organizing this area save me much time throughout the school year. Each August I devote upwards of a full week to planning out my entire homeschool year. Yes, the whole year.

   The first step in organizing a full year is planning my calendar and schedule. We roughly follow the public school calendar, and by that I mean we generally homeschool from September to May. We take long breaks when we need them and have the summers off. I have no qualms about taking full weeks or longer off from text work. Our schedule is a rough outline but also allows flexibility when we are all feeling like we need a break. We do a traditional four or five-day week but we also have sports on Saturdays, and then there is volunteering, the homeschool cooperative program and other activities. I don't worry much about specific time spent on homeschooling subjects but my state does require one-hundred and eighty days of homeschooling. We far exceed that amount both in the number of days and in hours spent on homeschooling.

• • •

Out of the Box Learning

Others choose to homeschool all year long, or work for several weeks and then take time off as needed. The hours that homeschoolers put in are probably far more than the required number of days or mandated hours. But most homeschoolers do not measure their learning by a calendar or by the number of days completed. Set hours and days are a measurement set by public schools, but don't often work well in the homeschool setting.

Calendar days are set for public schooled kids so that they are in compliance with compulsory attendance laws. The mindset is that children can, and will only learn while in school, and learning will only occur on a set number of days. Homeschoolers do not equate attendance with learning, and are never absent from homeschooling or learning.

Homeschoolers don't usually plan their learning based on calendar days, and this is puzzling to school officials who expect to see a concrete calendar where learning occurs on set days. Some parents start their school year in January, some in September and others do not even have start and stop dates, and instead, move seamlessly from one learning experience to another. When a curriculum or experience is finished, they simply move on to the next.

Promotion to the next grade level in public school means that you have satisfactorily learned everything you were supposed to in the prior grade. Unlike homeschoolers, public schools only promote to the next grade en masse. There is no moving ahead with curriculum, or advancing a grade or skill level, except at set times of the year, or in rare instances. Homeschoolers have the opportunity of moving to the next best thing when they ready. If a child is using a fourth grade text book and finishes it in six weeks, they move on to the next level regardless of what "grade" they may be in.

Homeschoolers do not usually take vacations when public school children are on vacation. Zoos, museums and other community places become overrun with children during public school vacations, and the learning experiences are deficient as the businesses deal with crowd control. We can visit the museum and zoo any time we choose and will likely get one-on-one tours and more information for our children, because the numbers are fewer. Homeschoolers are also available during the daytime hours, when other students are not. However, for my own sanity, I do schedule in a long break over Christmas and New Years, and about every six weeks we take a full week off just to regroup and breathe.

Once I know the rough calendar schedule for the year, I can begin to plan each child's outline. For yearly planning, I begin by taking the time to go through each child's textbooks table of contents to review the whole book. You don't need to read the whole book yet, but do familiarize yourself with the layout, material to be covered and what the sequence of assignments might be. Check for chapter tests or questions and note how they are formatted.

Usually the first five chapters of any text are review from the previous year, and the last five will be reviewed at the start of next year. You will find this is mostly true up until the high school years when subjects such as math and English become specialized into specific courses like Algebra and American or British Literature. In our ten years of homeschooling we have never once finished a full curriculum, with the exception of math. The math program we use is mastery based, not grade level based, so once the child has mastered the required skills, they move on to the next level.

Once I have the texts in my hands, I spend time browsing the chapters to see what we've already covered and what still needs to be covered. Some public school text books are divided into thirty-six lessons — the exact number of weeks of public school. That makes it easier to cover one chapter a week if you follow a traditional schedule. I cross out what I don't want to cover, or have already covered, and make small notes about things I'd like to expand within the lesson. For example, are there DVD's or field trips that can be incorporated into this lesson? Is there someone in our community that can provide insight and more personal information on this subject? Would interviewing them be helpful? Expand on any subject with whatever tools you think appropriate.

Out of the Box Learning

If a text has more than thirty-six chapters, feel free to break them down into the number you need to cover. If you homeschool all year long, you might cover less than a chapter each week. For my homeschool purposes, text books are merely guides to our learning. We skip chapters, move to other chapters, and essentially utilize the book in a way that makes sense for us, rather than go chapter by chapter in sequential order.

Once I have reviewed our texts and laid down a tentative plan, I create a spread-sheet for yearly planning. The first column is labeled week 1, week 2 etc. I don't put specific dates in the spread-sheet because if we change our vacation plans, it complicates the entire spreadsheet. Instead, we pick up on the week where we left off and I pencil in the dates or add them into my computer spread-sheet as we move through the weeks. As each week is completed, I highlight the entire line item to indicate it has been completed. I also separate the subjects into blocks and have columns for pages, chapter titles, textbook used and anything extra like vocabulary words.

A yearly plan might look like this:
Week 1-Lesson 1 Math Binomials text/pgs. 38-42/DVD Lesson 1.

Week 2-Lesson 2 Math Quadratic equations text/pgs. 45-52/DVD Lesson 2.

This format also allows us to be on various lesson numbers in different subjects. For instance, if math is taking more time than a typical week, lesson 1 may last for several weeks and I fill in the dates as we master the lesson. Lesson 1 might appear for weeks one, two and three, while science moves through each of the weeks in order. Week fourteen might have lesson twenty-three as an assignment if we decided to switch up the chapters, or if a child is excelling or needs more time to master the topic.

Beverly Burgess

I don't include specific assignments at this point, just the corresponding pages in the texts that need to be reviewed by the child or by me. Daily assignments will come later, but right now we're looking at the yearly plan. Again, feel free to skip anything that doesn't suit your needs. This method makes it easier to flip to the assignment to review it prior to teaching the kids. As their teacher, it is up to you to review any materials that your child will be learning about. You can't very well teach or facilitate a lesson if you haven't reviewed it, right?

Yearly planning is mostly for my use, so I can find the chapter and subject matter quickly, and to see if there are any materials or reading that I need to prepare. I do this with every text and subject, and for two children it takes me about six hours total to do everything for the whole year. Once completed, the same planning can be used in subsequent years for other children who may use the same text or lesson plans. Virtual lesson planning allows you to copy yearly assignments from one child to the next. If I have children in fifth and sixth grade, and in the following year my fifth grader moves up to the work that my sixth grader just completed, guess how much lesson planning I have to do? Zero! I simply copy and paste the full year of lessons into the current year's master list, assuming I'm still using the same curriculum.

The yearly planning also gives me a good idea of how much will be covered throughout each day and month. Some lessons need more review and others can be done much faster. Feel free to adjust accordingly, and know it will all work out as it needs to. Lesson 1 may actually last three weeks, but with my organizational method you can easily continue in any subject because it's planned out by lesson number or task, not specified weeks in which to be completed. If Lesson 1 takes three weeks, I can adjust that on the spreadsheet accordingly and still keep on track and move on to lesson 2 in other subjects.

Lesson Plans

New homeschoolers tend to panic at the thought of creating lesson plans. Planning does not need to strike fear in your hearts, and can be rather simplistic. Sunday is usually my lesson planning day, and for two children it takes me about one and a half hours to plan for both kids for the week, if I've done my yearly lesson planning thoroughly. For me, this includes reading any material or texts that need review or reading. With the yearly planning done, I can easily glance through the associated worksheets or questions and give the assignment to the children. Some parents just pick up on the next lesson and don't do any formal planning at all. It just depends on where your comfort zone is.

I use an online lesson manager called (HST) Homeschool Tracker (www.homeschooltracker.com) to manage courses and daily assignments. There is a very small monthly fee for HST that is worth every penny to me. HST allows me to catalog all my texts, chapter books, assign grades, complete lesson plans, document field trips, courses and subjects, and enter grades if needed. With the "Pro" version, I'm also able to create professional highschool transcripts that include GPA's, credits and course history with the click of a button. HST also allows you to transfer, save and copy assignments from one child to another, or even from one year to another. The assignment sheet section that I print for my kids is where I add in things such as reminders for papers, notes from me, outlines that are due or how and where I want science experiments recorded, or projects completed. I can also include any vocabulary lists, upcoming quizzes, tests, website links, MD appointments, sports practice times, or anything that might change our day's schedule.

Every Sunday, I enter the child's assignments for each day of the week into HST. The assignments show exactly which resource they will be using, (text, website, video, vocabulary, DVD etc.) along with the page numbers, problems, and questions to complete. I can also assign the order in which I want the subjects completed, but I usually let the kids decide what they want to tackle first.

An assignment might look like this:

Monday 5/14/15
Math

- Read pages 136-138.
- Watch lesson 6 on DVD.
- Do problems 1-5 with mom, complete problems 6-15 on your own.
- Be sure to show all of your work.
- Correct your work using the answer key. Review with mom.

My middle school child completes most of the work on the day assigned but will sometimes move ahead. My highschooler receives her assignments on Monday, and knows that everything must be completed and on my desk by Friday for me to review. What time frame she uses to complete this work is not my concern. Often, she will choose to work longer hours on Monday, Tuesday and Wednesday, and take Thursday and Friday off. She is the manager of her own time, and this skill is excellent time management preparation for college bound students.

Lesson planning is also the time for you, the teacher, to see what materials you need for the week. There is nothing worse than giving an assignment only to find out you needed art supplies for a project, or baking soda for a science experiment, and don't have the supplies on hand. Review tasks at least a week in advance to make sure you have everything that you need.

You can also create lesson plans that overlap subject areas, which is what I usually do. For instance, if we are studying ancient Rome, the history and the language arts portion might be to write an essay about what school was like in ancient Rome. Math is incorporated to include Roman numerals, and the science portion might be the study of the aqueduct system. Don't feel that every subject needs to be covered every single day. We do math and language arts every day, but science, history and foreign language twice a week. Neither of my kids particularly enjoy art or music in the traditional format, so we have found other things that interest them.

If you are not using an online program, a simple planning calendar or spiral notebook will suffice. There is nothing wrong with notes that say, "Math pgs. 4-10". Do what works best for you. Still, other parents choose to write the assignments down that they have completed after the work is done. They find this method less stressful than full lesson planning, and just choose the next lesson in the book and mark it down when completed. This method works well for unschoolers too, since they may use a variety of learning experiences besides textbooks.

I do not plan out how much time is spent on each subject. Public schools have their day divided by time increments because they have to manage thirty children in a classroom. Spending thirty minutes on math isn't helpful if the child needs more time to understand a concept. At the same time, if the child understood the concept and finished the assignment in only ten minutes, why not move on to the next chapter or a different topic entirely?

Beverly Burgess

Parents sometimes feel a need to homeschool for as many hours as public school is in session. They may fill this time with busy work, because they've been conditioned to think that school should take six hours per day. Let the children take as much or as little time as they need to master the goals of your homeschool. If any concept causes a parent or child to cry, throw it out or save it for another day when the child is more ready to tackle the topic. Just like grading, lesson plans should not be the measure of success as home educators. Use your lesson plans as a means for opportunity, rather than a measure of your teaching skill or your child's learning.

A new homeschooling parent stopped into my office one day, because she was struggling with the homeschool schedule she created for her children. They were burnt out and not wanting to do any homeschool work. She showed me the following:

 9:00-9:05 Morning pledge
 9:05-9:45 Morning circle/reading
 9:45-10:45 Language Arts
 10:45-11:45 Math
 11:45-12:15 Lunch
 12:15-12:45 Science
 12:45-1:15 Music/Art
 1:15-2:15 Language Arts
 2:15-3:15 Math

I asked her why she was requiring her children to follow a public school schedule and assigning times to complete the work. I told her to throw out the schedule for one month to see how things went, and to tackle no more than three subjects per day. She emailed a few weeks later and said her kids were so much more relaxed, and so was she — now that they weren't tied to the house or a strict schedule.

Remember as homeschoolers, you still have a household to run, meals to prepare; someone will get sick, you will have to make a trip to the doctor's office, or even the grocery store. Inevitably, it becomes impossible to stick to a strict schedule. The schedule becomes a kill-joy and ends up running your life.

I rise around 5:30 a.m., so that I have time to answer emails, shower, write, and browse social media over a cup of coffee. The kids get up about 7:30 a.m., eat breakfast, and complete all their chores before we begin our day. School work can begin anywhere around 8:00 a.m. or 8:30 a.m., and we usually work until about 11:30 a.m. or noon when we break for lunch. Their school work is most times done by noon, so the rest of the afternoon is theirs to do what they like. Some mornings they sleep in and we homeschool later in the day too.

My highschooler may work longer hours depending on whether a project or paper is due. There are days that we forgo our schoolwork to go to the park to meet with friends, and then adjust the school work to another day. A full homeschool day may be spent at the museum, and doesn't necessarily just include book work. We're out of the house more than we are home, but lessons can be done in the car or by utilizing a homeschool cooperative program, or anything in the community. Flexibility is key, and your homeschooler will likely complete much more work than you realize.

During the winter months, we tend to complete lots of book work because the weather is inclement, or it's too cold to go to the park. Conversely, we do far less book work during months when the weather is good. A nature walk can provide a richer learning experience than a text book lesson can. A day of fishing provides time with my kids to reconnect, and to have some deeper conversations that we would not be able to have if they were in school all day. All of our homeschooling efforts enhance family ties, strengthen our bonds, and create incredible self-esteem and self-reliance, along with fantastic learning experiences.

Once the kids have their weekly assignments, they are fairly independent in their work. I give written assignments starting around age seven. Even if kids reading skills are not fully developed,

I review each assignment with them to encourage the habit of taking charge of their learning in the coming years. If you are teaching multiple grades, teaching your kids how to be independent in their school work will be far less stressful for you, as their teacher, and for them as students. Parents are often surprised at how much more guiding and facilitating there is with homeschooling, rather than the preconceived amounts of teaching.

When homeschoolers need to review a new concept, it often takes just a few minutes with each child for them to understand the idea. Some concepts may take longer to teach as we work through math problems on the dry erase board, or work to outline a paper. Generally, new concepts are taught and learned quite fast in the homeschool setting, as you are not waiting for twenty to thirty kids to catch up, or to move ahead when they understand the subject matter. If school work is taking you as long as would in public school, then you are likely trying to cover too much material, or might even be giving too much instruction.

As Patrick moved up through the various grades and skill levels, the change in his work was remarkable. He went from a child pulled out of public school in fourth grade who could only complete two math problems, to independently learning and completing algebra, biology and a host of other subjects. He loved marine sciences for a while, so we did a full semester on a marine biology curriculum with lab work. We took field trips to local marine rescue groups, took a whale watching trip where he was able to help steer the boat with the captain, and talked extensively with the marine biologists on board about whale baleen. He wrote reports on what he learned, and it ended up being one of the most fulfilling and enriching topics we ever covered, most of which did not come from a textbook.

Trust that your children will make progress, especially if they have come from an educational setting that was a struggle for them. Help them in their learning but do not take over. Help them create independence in their learning from the start.

Determining Progress

What parents are asking when they inquire about testing is, "How can I be sure my child is learning?" Homeschooling parents spend a lot of time with their children and so they are best able to know when a child is learning. If we think back to our own public school experiences, we'd barely remember any of our testing or lessons. Much of that material was memorized so that we could pass the test. We would study for the test, hopefully pass it, and then not care if the material was remembered. The focus, at least when I was in school, was on the final grade.

When you homeschool, merely passing a test, does not equal learning. In fact, some parents choose not to test at all. Homeschoolers absorb learning all around them, and most times not during a test. Testing focuses on the result rather than the process or deep learning experiences. The completion of a chapter or unit test in homeschooling, does not end the learning of topics and skills that children are invested in.

From kindergarten through the end of the middle school years, I don't grade work much at all. There is a difference between reviewing a child's work and grading it. Actual grades really aren't necessary when you teach for mastery, and when working one-on-one with your child. Grading work is a benefit to the teacher, not the child. As the teacher, you know that if your child finishes a worksheet of twenty problems and completes twelve incorrectly, that you need to review the material again. The questions that a child completed in error, are easily corrected by pointing out what parts are done correctly, and where they started to go astray. A simple, "Let's review this part again," is usually all that is needed for mastery.

Oftentimes when working with Patrick in math, he would complete part of the problem correctly, but then lose his way in multiple step problems that resulted in the wrong answer. By acknowledging what parts he did correctly, I was able to easily remedy any areas where more review was needed, and have him rework the problems from the last thing he got right.

A child's individual development also determines how well they test. Patrick did not learn his multiplication tables until eighth grade. This was a major problem for him in public school, and his teacher felt I was lax in assuring he learned his math facts, when other students were required to learn them in fourth grade. We studied his times-tables almost daily but it didn't help. There was some disconnect in his brain that no matter what we did, those darn facts just wouldn't stick. I knew he understood the concept of multiplication, but memorization just didn't work for him. Timed math tests stressed him out and the quick responses required at public school were not something he could manage. We used a multiplication table reference sheet whenever he needed it both in public school, and when we completed work at home. It drove his public school teachers over the edge, because the memorization of facts was a required skill. However, we insisted that Patrick be accommodated on his IEP to be allowed to use a multiplication table anytime it was needed. We also had them remove all timed testing and any tests that were only math facts. It didn't serve much purpose to take a test on math facts using a multiplication table. The added exposure to the multiplication table and continued practice eventually led him to memorize the facts when he was developmentally ready. Now that he's in college, no one ever asks him when he learned his multiplication facts, or at what age he learned to read. By giving him time to mature and by using a system that worked for him, we saved him a lot of frustration.

Once my kids reach the highschool years, I do give them letter/numerical grades and credits. It is still up to the homeschool parent to review their homeschooler's work. If my highschooler fails a test or assignment, then we have to sit and review it again until mastery is achieved. Parents wonder if allowing them to retest is beneficial since a homeschooled child would technically then receive all A's. My feeling is that homeschooling is the time to correct them and let them retry, so that they can master the skills and study habits they will need for college and later life. Why wouldn't you let them try again?

My children each have their own assignment binder. Each Sunday, their assignments for the whole week are placed in their three-ring binder with the most recent week on top. The kids check off their assignments as they are completed. For younger children, it is important that you review this week's work to ensure understanding of the assignment. Younger kids often do not fully read directions and sometimes miss parts of assignments. You can highlight the subjects or the days of the week, in different colors to help them better visualize the assignment and to keep them organized. If you have young kids that are not yet reading, try using pictures of what you want them to accomplish. A photo of their story book with a check off mark works great! If tackling science, you can use a picture of seed planting or whatever you will cover that week and have them mark off when finished.

At the completion of each year, I remove the full year's assignments and file them in a manila folder, labeled with the child's name, grade and year. I keep these for three years and then toss them. Records for highschool students should be saved for all four years. Should any school officials ever question any of our work, subjects covered or the amount of days in attendance, I have a good record of what has been completed. The saved folders are also a great reminder for those days when you are feeling like you haven't done enough. Pull out a completed yearly packet and glance through it. Feel good about how much you and your children have accomplished!

Some states require you to submit work samples or portfolios for your children as a means to show progress, but papers and completed work can quickly get out of hand. I have a large basket on my desk that all completed work, (except computer work) gets put into. The basket system is more efficient during the elementary school years than upper grades. Each Friday I go through all the work and pick out one paper from each subject. Try to pick papers that will show progress in each subject or topic area you are studying. Yes, that means showing both lack of understanding and mastery of topics.

For instance, if you are working on two-digit multiplication, choose a paper that shows the child's initial work at the start of learning, and then one where mastery was achieved. Ten to twelve papers from each subject for the whole year, should suffice for a well-rounded sample work portfolio. Be sure to include art projects, notes from music teachers or mentors, or others your child may have learned from. Instead of saving every art project and paper, I take photos of the art and completed work, and add that to the portfolio. It saves not only space, but time, and is an outstanding way to keep memories without the clutter. Include any certificates of achievement, or notes of thanks for community service work too. Many of these are acceptable methods of recording your school year if your portfolio needs to be reviewed by any school officials.

Scrapbooking is also a great way to document the homeschool year. During the first year that we homeschooled, I created a beautiful album of photos, work samples and odds and ends about field trips. I kept the ticket stubs from events and the pretty leaves we collected from nature walks and included those in the album too. It was great to show relatives (or the naysayers that asked, "So what did you guys do this year?" The grandparents were delighted to flip through the pages to see all that the kids accomplished. Each year they began to look forward to seeing the book, not so much to calm to their fears, but to truly rejoice in a year where their grandchildren thrived.

On a few occasions, the grandparents even attended zoo field trips and were included in the photos. Reminiscing with the kids about time spent together became a favorite activity and a way for them to share in this miraculous journey. If you are on a tight budget, request that birthday or holiday gifts include passes to museums or zoos, or maybe some classes that your children would like to take. Asking grandparents to purchase the tickets and attend with you is a tremendous way to include them in your child's homeschooling. Rather than fill your house up with more plastic toys and gifts, the grandparents or aunts or uncles will be giving your children the opportunity of experiences and exploration. Documenting your homeschool days with family and friends is a wonderful reminder for those days when you feel like you are not doing enough.

Standardized testing may be required by your state laws. Homeschooled students do not usually find standardized testing helpful. In essence, the testing tells you how your child did answering the correct number of questions compared to those children in the same grade level. If your child is at various grade levels, standardized testing will not give you an accurate picture of how your child is progressing, only where they are in comparison to other kids in the expected grade. Think about how standardized tests are graded. Scores are usually given in percentiles, meaning your child scored better or worse than a certain number of other children in the same grade. It sounds innocent enough but your child may not be learning the same things as their public school counterparts or even using the same curriculum. Is it fair to test children on material that they are not familiar with, or haven't yet covered when they may be at various grade levels?

For homeschoolers, a poor standardized test score likely does not mean your child is doing poorly, but that they simply are covering different material at a different time and rate, then the children in public school. Standardized testing can be done in a variety of ways if your state requires it. Most districts will provide testing opportunities, so that homeschoolers can take the testing when public schooled children do. Other states will allow parents to administer the tests, and then allow either the testing company or parents to send results to the district. Still, other states that require testing, do not necessarily require the test scores to be sent to any school official at all. Some parents feel that the actual taking of the test is a benefit, and that timed testing and interpreting questions, prepares students for future testing outside of the home.

Like most other things, practice and a full explanation to the children about timed tests are usually all that is needed should the situation arise. Kids are resilient and thinking that they can't take a test, or figure out directions is ill-founded. I would much rather a child take his/her time and give well thought out answers, rather than trying to choose the "most correct" answer. Trick questions or questions with multiple correct answers, do not teach children deciphering or analytical thinking skills.

Most standardized testing administered by school districts is also common core aligned. Since we know that the curriculum is also aligned so kids can past the test, we cannot expect a student who has not been taught with the same curriculum to do well. It is often said that common core is not a curriculum, but rather a series of benchmarks for students to achieve. Almost all public education textbooks are now common core aligned. If you purchase a curriculum from a major text manufacturer, and they align their text to common core national standards, you then have a national curriculum in which students must be taught to pass the test. There is no other way but to produce the answers that are prescribed by the curriculum.

Out of the Box Learning

The testing becomes a direct measure of the curriculum, which becomes a measure of children's learning.

The A to F grading scale that most of us are familiar with at public schools, forces kids to move on to the next skill without mas-tery. In some instances, they may have to repeat a whole grade level or class if they fail. The result is that students are often required to relearn, the whole subject or course, in its entirety all over again, even if some understanding of the topic was gained. Instead of re-viewing the missed concepts, children must repeat an entire year or subject or attend summer school. The probability is high, that the students will be disengaged while "relearning" material that has al-ready been, at least partially mastered.

Homeschooling provides a far better approach to both testing and evaluating mastery than in the public schools. During the high school years, the kids and I talk about our work daily and I can easily discern if they have merely skimmed the material, or if they have done some in depth reading, critical thought and further research. Since kids in the upper grades tend to work more independently, most of their work consists of essays or research papers. Multiple choice or write in answers do little for me as their teacher nor for the student, in recognizing whether material has been learned. Most of the questions only require memorization, or that one exact word to fill in the blank.

Testing can have its place. My approach to chapter tests is simply using them as a chapter summary. By the time we get to the chapter test, my homeschooled children should have thoroughly mastered the concepts presented to them. If I know that they are still struggling with the material, I'm not going to give the chapter test just because it's the end of the chapter. I also don't feel a need to give any test if I've been working with my student, and it's clear they understand the concepts by the work they have already pro-duced. Why give a test when you are already clear that they under-stand? Nothing is worse than a child completing a research project

Beverly Burgess

that includes dioramas, written and oral reports, citing resources, and then telling them you are going to test them on their knowledge.

The same holds true for any subject, but especially in math. Have their worksheets been mostly correct to indicate understanding, or have they learned the material some other way? If so, there is no need to test just for the sake of completing the test, or feeling like should do it. Working with your children each day, you will have a very clear understanding of where their strengths and weaknesses are, and where you need to spend more time on concepts.

Alternate Ways to Learn

Children are often required to learn American History for nine or more years throughout their public education. That is completely unnecessary in homeschooling and really for any child. Can you imagine spending nine years of your life studying the same subject over and over again, with only minute or unimportant details added? History can easily be taught in one year in the middle school years. While our nation's history is important, should my kids come across something they are unfamiliar with, it is easily researched or found on the internet as we do with all other things in life.

Field trips to historic places are a great way for kids to learn at the elementary level. They provide a first-hand look at how the people of the time lived and the challenges they faced, rather than just reading about it in a text. We have switched things up by studying geography or Ancient Rome, and even a unit study on the underground railroad by incorporating our own family genealogy in the process. I am not overly concerned with history that happened two-hundred years ago either. Is one event that happened centuries ago more important than current events? Not in our house. Certainly we do cover some basic history, but I'm more concerned with teaching my children what is going on in the world now, and how to make a difference, rather than dwell on the inaccurate history of our past. My feeling is that as parents, we need to provide our children with modern challenges of the world and help them develop, thought processes to problem solve, if they are to contribute today's world.

Public school requires children be in school for more than fourteen years, if you include preschool and kindergarten. Homeschooling allows us to advance our children as needed, and to combine grades, or finish our formal schooling much faster than public school does. Middle school can be completed in one year, many elementary grades can be combined quite easily, and highschool need not take four years with a set plan and required courses. Think out of the box when it comes to your children's education. Are they excelling in some areas? Move them ahead, graduate them early, don't require the normal K-12 grades. Be adventurous and follow your own path in their learning.

The Highschool Years

It is always difficult to see how our society treats teenagers, and all children really. They are blamed for everything from vandalism, to the total demise of the world as we know it. They are criticized for using technology, and then told to use technology to advance the world. We criticize them for their hairstyles and their choice of clothing, and tell them they make poor decisions. Yet we don't allow them time and space to develop their own self-awareness and authentic selves. We tell them to be independent, but give them none of the tools to accomplish independence.

In my experience, teens are fabulous and they do make good decisions when they are empowered and allowed to do so. It is the very essence of teens to try to explore and to figure out adult thinking. It is also necessary for teens to make mistakes and choose pathways, that as parents, we wouldn't necessarily choose. Hopefully your homeschooling teens will more readily come to you to about big decisions, both before and after they happen. The hope is that they will give good thought and care to each new challenge that is in front of them. The high school years are a critical time in a child's development when they are trying to bridge the gap between their youth and adult hood. Decisions about part-time work and colleges, and even tender relationships all need a parent's guidance and homeschooling is the perfect place to allow that to happen.

In contrast, public school teens will often turn away from their parents, and instead look to their peers for advice on dating and other important decisions. Teens who can share concerns and important decisions with their parents, are better able to make larger life decisions when they leave home. Confiding and turning to their parents doesn't mean that they don't have social interactions with other teens. It just means that strong family foundations have been built, and homeschooled teens are more apt to come to talk to their parents about an issue.

At the very time when parental involvement is most needed during the highschool years, is when I see a lot of parents panic and send their kids back to public school. The parents begin to worry about prom and student council, and if their child will even be able to get into college. They worry whether they will be able to teach higher math or sciences, and assume it is too hard, or beyond their own understanding. Homeschooling through highschool is no more difficult or easy than any other grade. I hear, "I'll homeschool up to eighth grade and then we'll enroll them in public school because they need those highschool experiences." What highschoolers need is appropriate age experiences, and opportunities to work those challenges out both independently and with their parents help and wisdom.

When Patrick was moving from tenth to eleventh grade, he decided to go to a local charter school. Reflecting back on that time, I was not confident in my ability to teach him the higher math courses, or really anything except science, (because of my nursing background) and so we pushed him to attend. My husband was still struggling with the idea of homeschooling too, mostly in the sense of our son succeeding academically. Neither of us had been through any part of getting a homeschooled child into college and were quite intimidated, so we allowed him to return to a public charter school.

Out of the Box Learning

In retrospect, we should have called on our homeschool community to help us navigate our questions about homeschooling and college, but instead we questioned our own skills and ability to parent our child. While Patrick did mostly well during his time at the charter school, we all struggled with the public school structure and strict guidelines on testing. Things like being on the National Honor Society and obtaining straight A's, yet failing his standardized testing — jeopardized his graduation date. The academics were not an issue, but rather the rules and regulations surrounding what was considered success in those subjects.

Patrick did graduate on time, although it took several meetings with the school and several more attempts at taking the standardized test, to pass in time for graduation. After graduation, he was accepted to all six colleges he applied to, but chose to attend a small liberal arts college in New England as a writing major. This child, who left public school and started out in homeschool not able to write a complete sentence, or finish more than two math problems in fourth grade; who worked his way through years of homeschooling and a charter school, was now succeeding on every level at college. Now, he writes twenty page papers, devours literature and wants to become a professor. Larry and I learned a lot through this process; mostly to trust ourselves in fully equipping our children with everything they need to excel and learn. And because of what we learned, our daughter is remaining home for her highschool years and we couldn't be more excited!

Homeschooling through highschool can be done, and the years are not so scary. Have confidence in your child's ability to learn and in your ability as their parent and teacher. There are many resources to help homeschoolers through the highschool years — if you don't give up before you start!

Let's talk about the nitty gritty of what homeschooling looks like during the highschool years, and where to find resources to help you on this path. By the highschool years, teens should be fairly independent in their learning. My highschooler gets her assignments on Monday for the week and they must be completed and on my desk for me to correct by Friday. She comes to me when she needs help understanding a concept, or when she needs further explanation. Usually ten or fifteen minutes spent at the beginning of each Monday, to review the week's work and expectations is all that is needed. If we need to spend more time during the week to help her understand a concept, that's okay too.

Throughout the day, a discussion on the material read, further brief instructions and help when asked for, is enough to evaluate understanding and get them on their way for the week.

Because teens are so independent in their work, that usually means that they will be the ones teaching themselves the more difficult, "I can't possibly teach this" subjects, not you. If you think having your child teach themselves seems like a terrible way educate them, I would say, that you are providing the opportunity to figure something out for themselves. That is an invaluable skill in preparing them for later life decisions. How much time do you think a college professor is going to spend with your child with 1:1 tutoring? And if they do need help, what will they do or where will they turn? Your children will need to work that out for themselves in college, and highschool is a great place to practice.

We have always been able to find someone in our community, or through online resources, who can help when the going gets tough. Don't be afraid to turn to the answer key or teacher manual when you are stuck. Sometimes working backwards through the problem, or viewing the exact steps needed to solve the problem or question, helps get you over that hump. This is especially true in math. Look at an answer or two, and see if you can complete the rest of the worksheet or pages now that you have some guidance on how to solve the problem.

The homeschooled high school course of study does not in any way need to resemble that of public school. This can be a very freeing thing to a child when a commonly covered subject is not

Out of the Box Learning

required, or is approached in a completely different way. Homeschooled highschool students get to choose courses, areas of focus, assign credits and develop a portfolio unique to their skills, interests and talents. My main focus during the highschool years is always writing, researching, and basic highschool level math skills. For us, if you can master those things well, you can find out just about anything else in the world that you want to learn about. Colleges adore and readily recruit homeschoolers, or out of the box thinking kids, and any transcript or portfolio that provides a unique approach to skill mastery, is bound to get attention. Unique kids make unique applicants to college!

Homeschooling through the highschool years also means that you as the parent, get to assign credits. If your child is an avid piano player and practices many hours a day, and you want to give them two credits per year for piano, you can do that. If your child is completing an apprenticeship with an engineer, and you want to give them five credits — you can do that too. Homeschooling during the highschool years means your child's interests and activities are counted as part of the curriculum, rather than in addition to it. This approach means you don't have to try to come up with a list of electives just to fill the schedule or credit requirements.

You should also remember that highschool courses, or any grade level for that matter, can be completed in any length of time. Public schools usually split credit hours into a half semester or year-long credit. So a half credit for a half year course is given, and a full credit is given for a full year class. These are usually based on the number of hours completed within the course to receive the full credit value. Homeschoolers can complete chosen courses on their own time frame, rather than determine completion based on calendar dates. Does it matter more that you spent a full year on a course, or just that you mastered it in whatever time frame necessary?

I had one homeschooler in our group who was unschooled for his entire life, but in what would have been his junior year; mastered and completed algebra in three short weeks. The higher maths including algebra II, physics and calculus were completed in the same manner. This homeschooler, who waited until he felt a need to tackle these subjects and was truly interested in them, was well equipped to complete all four courses in just one year's time as opposed to a regular highschool course of study spanning four years. He also tackled these subjects when he was very clear on what he wanted to do in college, and learned that higher math was a requirement for the program he wanted to enter. This student graduated from homeschool in what would have been his junior year, because he completed all the requirements with his own determination, and by what the college he was applying to required of him. He started full-time college almost a year ahead of schedule, and went on to challenge out of college classes and complete his education far sooner than anyone expected.

Homeschoolers who need more time to master concepts can take the time to do so without having to worry about getting through a chapter based on a calendar schedule. Those free to learn on their own terms are not plagued with endless hours of homework either, nor any homework or busy work at all, for that matter. In public school, homework is given to support the lessons of the day, to give students extra practice, and sometimes just because the district says homework must be given. Even if a student has full understanding of a subject or topic they must still complete homework. Because homeschoolers are able to complete their work much faster and with greater understanding, homework becomes unnecessary. There is no busy work, only deep down concentrated learning.

There are more ways than ever before to help you homeschool your child through the highschool years. The internet is filled with an abundance of material, resources and online classes that can help your student learn about most anything. Homeschool cooperatives are another great option for team learning, and your local homeschool group is the place to connect and pool resources in learning. Remember that you are never alone in this process.

Out of the Box Learning

Subjects like foreign languages or music lessons can be learned with online distance tutors. We have several homeschooled students using this method now and they communicate via online video chatting. It's like having the teacher right in the room with you. Some of our parents are even learning right along with their kids. What better way to show a love of lifelong learning then to learn right beside your children?

Homeschooling through highschool does not have to be intimidating, but it does help to have a plan. Credit planning or portfolio creation should begin in eighth grade for your highschool years. Be flexible in this area — this is a rough outline and things can be changed as you make your way through each year. No course needs to be studied in a specific year, and subjects like biology or earth science do not need to be followed in the traditional order. Some homeschoolers never formally study these subjects, yet have been readily accepted to college. Depending on your major, colleges may require a portfolio of work. When Patrick declared his writing major, the colleges asked for a writing portfolio; not because he was homeschooled, but because it was a requirement of the program he chose. He included longer essays, critical analysis papers, poetry, and some creative writing. He also had to submit an essay from a list of topics supplied by the college. It was a great way for the college to see his skill level and his commitment to writing.

Depending on what state you live in, there might be a specific number of credits required for graduation. Some public schools will give diplomas to homeschoolers based on explicit documentation and testing to prove learning. In general, homeschool parents issue the diploma, and there are few colleges who won't accept homeschoolers. Credits can vary across the board, but in general they are broken down in core subjects like the ones listed below. Credits can vary whether you are on a college track, which usually requires a higher number of credits, or a general graduation diploma which may not require as many credits as a college track student.

TYPICAL COURSE OF STUDY FOR HIGH SCHOOL HOMESCHOOLERS

Highschool Subject Area	Typical Credits College Bound	Non College Bound
English	4 credits (English I, II, III, IV) Consider American and British courses	4 credits
Mathematics	4 credits • Algebra I • Geometry • Algebra II • Calculus and/or Trigonometry • Consumer/Business Math	4 credits Higher math may or may not be needed.
History	4 credits • U.S. History & Geography. • World History, culture, and Geography. • American Government/ Civics. • Economics.	4 credits
Science	4+ credits • Physical Sciences • Environmental Science • Chemistry • Physics Labs for each subject above may be ½ credit each	3-4 credits + 1 credit lab
Foreign Language	2-3 credits • No dead languages (Latin). • Take same language all years.	0 credits Some colleges may accept or offer Latin.
Arts	3 credits • Visual and Performing Arts (Glee Club, Band, Theater, Art, etc.)	1 credit
Physical & Health Education	2 credits (1/4-1/2 credit each year)	1-2 credits
Electives	2-3 credits • Computer Programming/Sciences. • Yearbook • Art • Photography etc.	2 credits
Total	23-26 credits	22-23 credits

SAMPLE COURSE SCHEDULE

The sample schedule below represents the typical 21-26 credits needed for graduation from high school. College-bound students typically graduate with 24-26 credits. These additional credits can include AP courses, computer technology courses, advanced study, or courses in other areas of interest.

GRADE 9

World Geography	1 Credit
Biology with Lab	1.5 Credits
Literature & Composition 1	1 Credit
Algebra 1	1 Credit
Fine Art/Electives	1 Credit
Health & Physical Education	½ Credit
Foreign Language	1 Credit

6.5-7.0 credits

GRADE 10

World History	1 Credit
Environmental Science	1 Credit
Literature & Composition II	1 Credit
Geometry	1 Credit
Fine Arts/Electives	1 Credit
Health & Physical Education	½ Credit
Foreign Language	1 Credit

6.5 credits/13.5 credits total

GRADE 11   GRADE 12

Grade 11	Credits	Grade 12	Credits
Chemistry with Lab	1.5 Credits	Physics	1 Credit
American Literature	1 Credit	borderWorld Literature	1 Credit
Algebra II	1 Credit	Calculus or Trigonometry	1 Credit
U.S. History/U.S. Government	1 Credit	Economics	1 Credit
Foreign Language	1 Credit	Foreign Language	1 Credit
Electives	1-2 Credits	Electives	1-2 Credits

6.5 credits/20 credits total   **6.0 credits/26 credits total**

- Full year courses =1 credit per full year course/120-180 hours of work.
- Lab courses = ½ credit (usually ½ year but may be a full year long). 60 hours of work.
- Health & Physical Education=1/2 credit for one full year.
- Electives= ½ credit for ½ year, full credit for full year.
- Consider AP classes in Junior/Senior year or dual college enrollment.

Out of the Box Learning

I cannot stress enough to find a software program to keep track of all that your child completes and that will help you create a professional looking transcript. There are downloads available from the internet that make it easy for parents and highschoolers to fill in their course credit information, and allow you to easily calculate GPA's. Consultants are also available to help you organize and create your transcripts if this process seems overwhelming to you. If you handwrite your transcript, colleges won't give you a second glance and they will not accept this format as an official document. Include the following information when creating your transcript.

- Name, DOB, address, phone and email.
- If college bound, include expected graduation date from highschool.
- Listing of completed, or expected courses to be completed.
- Grades for each course/GPA.
- Include labs and credits.
- Include all electives with added description (think job resume'.)
- Include PSAT/SAT/ACT scores/standardized testing.
- List of any other schools attended.
- Online classes/certificates of completion.
- College classes/attach official transcript.
- Further activities/achievements (Eagle Scouts, National Honor Society, etc.)
- Don't forget volunteerism, odd jobs, work experience, computer skills.

Begin your college search early to determine entry requirements. For example, some colleges require anyone with a GED or homeschool diploma, to have two years of community college classes, before admission is granted to their college or university. My personal recommendation is to look elsewhere if this is a requirement. Placement tests and a portfolio should satisfy any college in their need to understand if your child is a viable candidate, or capable of completing college level work. Most colleges do not and should not require a GED for admission. A GED implies that your student has not completed course work and nothing is farther from the truth for homeschoolers. Your transcript should suffice at any college.

Some colleges or chosen majors will not accept creation sciences as coursework. Be sure you know what colleges require before you apply, and if you are lacking in any areas, use the highschool years to complete those obligations.

If the college your homeschooler is applying to requires a portfolio, here are some things to include:
- Samples of written research papers.
- Samples of creative writing.
- Photos of volunteerism, learning expeditions with written explanations in job resume' format.
- Include one or two hobbies. Colleges want to see that you have other interests besides academics and where you might fit into and bring diversity to their college life offerings.
- Unschoolers may also need to provide course descriptions to the college. Even if your homeschooler chose an untraditional course, learn to work the course description into what the college needs for admission.

Many community colleges have dual enrollment programs for highschoolers and this is the route I see homeschoolers take most often. Dual enrollment allows highschoolers who have demonstrated academic achievement and maturity, to enroll in college while still in highschool. Having become independent in their school work, and invested in their learning, homeschoolers usually excel in college life. Dual enrollment allows homeschoolers to finish their highschool years faster, and then to begin and finish their college years at a much faster pace with far less debt. Core classes can be taken at the community college level and then easily transferred to four year universities, if students are looking to save money and complete basic requirements. Many homeschoolers just as easily matriculate directly into four year colleges in their highschool years. Some choose not to follow the community college path and instead, apply to the four-year college or university of their choice.

There's no secret formula when it comes to college admission decisions. Students and parents should know that many factors influence admission decisions, and every college has different requirements. Many small, selective colleges pay greater attention to personal statements and essays, letters of recommendation, leadership experiences and the individual talents of applicants. Ultimately, grades are important but the assumption is that if you are applying to college, you are capable of college work. Most other highschool students are going to have similar courses under their belts and likely similar grades. So anything you can do to stand out amongst the crowd will be well worth your time.

Colleges typically offer the chance for a face-to-face interview to really get to know the prospective student. Large, public state university systems often use a mathematical formula based on a student's grade point average (GPA), and scores on the SAT or ACT. In state, and out of state applicant percentages are sometimes based on a ratio. They may or may not offer in person interviews for the student.

Regardless of a college's evaluation system, your students should present a well-rounded picture of their skills, experiences and personal traits. Applications should highlight their ability to succeed at each particular institution and what they can contribute to student life on campus. The common application, has leveled the playing field, in that many colleges now receive the same information from the student. In some regards, it saves students time in filling out multiple applications to many different schools. On the other hand, there is little room for personalization, or for the student to stand out amongst their peers because the same information gets transmitted to all of your college choices.

The common application requires:
- A copy of your high school transcript.
- A list of your extracurricular activities both inside and outside of school.
- Test scores and test dates from your college entrance exam like SAT's, ACT scores, SAT subject test scores).
- Parent/legal guardian information including educational background, occupational information, employer information, etc.
- The essay question.

Some colleges are no longer requiring standardized test scores and instead, rely more heavily on the student's portfolio for a more global picture of the student. Personal statements and essays are both a measure of writing ability, and a window into each student's background. Colleges may require a personal essay in addition to the common app essay. Admission officers want to hear an original voice in the student's own words. When my son was accepted to all six colleges he applied to, the admissions directors put a large amount of emphasis on his personal essay. For a successful essay, encourage students to get to the point quickly and personalize their writing through specific examples, and to speak from personal experience. The essay that outlines your career goals in bullet points or states that your hero is your father, will quickly be passed over.

Out of the Box Learning

At selective colleges, strong support in the form of letters of recommendation will be needed too. Homeschooled students can obtain letters of recommendation from volunteer work experiences, clergy, employers, mentors, professors at college classes, cooperative classes or members of the community. The recommendations should be highly specific, describing not just each student's love of learning, but the ways in which the students have demonstrated that they can add to the classroom experience, challenge themselves, and attempt original projects and thinking. Evidence of nonacademic activities is important to the admission process as well, and depth of involvement is more impressive than breadth.

Students can achieve this if they:
- Focus on a limited number of interests. Do not include every single class ever taken or the karate class you took for three months.
- Document long-term involvement with organizations. Include monthly volunteerism at the soup kitchen and how long you have been involved with this organization. Long-term volunteerism, commitment to a cause, and involvement in organizations is especially appreciated, rather than volunteerism that is required just to meet a certain number of hours for school work or credit attainment.
- Highlight activities related to a major or career goal. Include apprenticeships or work study programs that gave the student first-hand experience. Perhaps your budding journalism major spent a summer being mentored by a reporter for the newspaper. They might have helped edit copy, or applied to the navy, or maybe they are already certified in deep sea diving.
- Show leadership skills and ability. Did your student lead youth groups, or design a class for homeschoolers?

Many colleges set aside admission spaces for students who may not meet traditional criteria, but who will add to class diversity and campus life. Geographic location, racial or ethnic background, extenuating or unusual life circumstances and experience living or studying overseas may all be influential. Evidence suggests that in some cases, applying for early decision may also increase the chances of admission, and may benefit in added financial aid awards.

Parents of college bound homeschooled students should begin their planning early. Take it year by year and do what you can in meeting requirements. This is by no means an exhaustive list, but it's a great start to getting you organized if your student is following the traditional path to college.

Freshman Year (Grade 9)

- Find an online program to begin your transcript, or create one using a spreadsheet.
- Research high school course requirements for several colleges you might attend. Be sure to investigate credits needed in foreign languages, maths, English and other subjects, and plan accordingly.
- Plan a tentative four-year course outline for high school. Begin your basic outline at end of grade eight.
- Explore career interests. Reach out to career counselors, or people in the field you are interested in, for help and assistance.
- Research which schools require SAT's for admission. Many schools have moved away from this practice and instead require portfolios. Check out (http://www.fairtest.org/university/optional), to see the requirements of the college you are interested in.

- Call colleges to clarify and verify requirements if unsure.
- Begin a list of church, sports, community service, and other extra-curricular activities, and especially note any leadership roles. Keep a file with records of these, including hours and your job/role in the organization, as well as any awards, letters of recommendation from employers or leaders of volunteer activities. Ask for letters of recommendation as service or projects are completed.
- Begin your transcript and update every year. Do not wait until you are in tenth or eleventh grade to complete this. Online programs or templates will work just fine for creating templates.
- Prepare a tentative budget for college by researching in state and out of state schools.
- Meet with college financial aid planners early, and consider part time work to meet future financial needs.
- Research PSAT classes over summer and schedule for fall.

Sophomore Year (Grade 10)

- Schedule your PSAT's in early fall. Testing occurs in October at local high schools or other locations. In most states, you must call your local district to schedule testing. Many districts only have a certain number of spaces for testing and need to order the tests well in advance of your scheduled date. Homeschoolers are often given these slots if any remain, after public schooled children are scheduled. If your state uses a digital format for testing, there may be more openings for your child to participate.

- Continue research on high school course requirements for several colleges you might attend.
- Revise your four-year plan for high school if needed.
- Begin to investigate potential colleges by planning visits and exploring scholarships. Note dates for early admission and scholarship deadlines.
- Explore career interests.
- Add to your list of church, sports, community service, and other extra-curricular activities, especially note any leadership roles. Keep a file with records of these, as well as any awards, letters of recommendation from employers or leaders of volunteer activities.
- Consider dual enrollment at a community college for junior year.
- Revise your transcript, adding this year's courses and grades and GPA.
- Prepare a tentative budget for high school and college.
- Consider part time work to meet future financial needs.
- Over the summer, research SAT's and schedule testing for fall.

Junior Year (Grade 11)
- Consider dual enrollment at a community college, or full enrollment at a four-year university/college while completing your highschool years.
- Research high school course requirements for several colleges you might attend.
- Revise your four-year plan for high school. Make sure you have all core classes covered as well as electives. Complete this as soon as possible.
- Investigate potential colleges by planning visits, scheduling interviews and exploring scholarships and financial aid.

Out of the Box Learning

- Note dates for early admission and scholarship deadlines.
- Visit colleges when in session, instead of while college is on break. Empty colleges do not provide a full picture of campus life. Dress for an interview in your most professional clothing. This is not a time for jeans or sweatpants but to present your most professional, best self. Ask to specifically tour the departments or buildings of majors you are interested in. Ask the admissions director if you might be paired with or interview a student studying your chosen major. Meet with the head of the department.
- Send a thank you note for your tour or interview. Note your areas of interest and what you liked about the campus and where you might fit in. Ask to schedule a follow-up phone call if you have more questions.
- Retake your SAT's if your scores were not adequate the first time.
- Attend a financial aid night at a local high school or through the College Board. Contact the Financial Aid Director at the colleges you are interested in, to explore scholarships, financial aid and work study programs.
- Begin work on your college essay. Do not wait to begin this! http://professionals.collegeboard.com/guidance/applications/essay
- Begin filling out the Free Application for Federal Student Aid/FAFSA form (https://fafsa.ed.gov/). Do not assume you will not qualify for financial aid. Homeschoolers qualify for the same financial aid as those students in public school.

Senior Year (Grade 12)

- Research high school course requirements for several colleges you might attend.
- Finalize your transcripts and have the official copy notarized.
- Apply to colleges for early admission or early decision if you wish. This is usually completed by November of your senior year.
- Be sure to review early admissions and decision requirements. If you accept early admission, some schools require you to withdraw the applications you submitted to other schools.
- You may not want to apply early, if you are relying on financial aid for school, or if you want to review multiple admissions and financial aid packets.
- Complete your common application and college essay(s). The common application is usually available August 1, to begin to work on. Be aware of your preferred college's, early and regular application deadlines. Most regular application deadlines are January 1.
- Consider an internship in your chosen field.
- Review acceptance letters from colleges. These are usually mailed during March and April.
- Financial award letters may come after acceptance letters — they usually arrive from February through April, and may you to help you make your determination on college choice.
- Make final college decisions and deposits by May 1.
- Celebrate your graduation with family and friends.
- Begin shopping for college needs. Most colleges have a list of basic needs to bring to campus.

Navigating financial aid and forms for college can be daunting. Most colleges have a window of time in which application fees are reduced or waived. Ask your chosen colleges to waive your application fees if possible, most will do so if asked.

FAFSA (Free Application for Federal Student Aid is available October 1, and should be filled out as soon as possible. Colleges divvy up grant, loan and scholarship money early in the year, so you want to be sure that you have the best chance of qualifying. All federal loans for students and parents require a completed FAFSA. Most schools will require a completed FAFSA form for any financial aid consideration including scholarships and grants, even if you are not using federal loans. Some schools may require additional financial aid forms, or supplemental forms, for hardship determination. Early application to colleges increases chances for grants and scholarships. Contact the college and let them know of any extra financial hardships. Many colleges will award more money based on need.

###

Senior Year Planning Month by Month

August Before Senior Year

Come up with a preliminary list of colleges that includes "reach schools," "match schools" and "safety schools." Reach schools are those that may be a stretch for you to attend based on finances or admission criteria. Match schools are those schools that fit most of your needs in terms of finances, majors and admission criteria. Safety schools are those schools that you are likely to be accepted to based on geographic area, finances or admission requirements.

Register for the September ACT/SAT if you have not already done so and be sure to check your credits to make sure you're taking the English, math, social science, science, and foreign language classes you'll need for your top-choice colleges. Depending on your major, this may vary greatly.

Look over the Common Application and begin thinking about potential topics for your personal essay. Most colleges will have sample questions posted to their website for you to explore. Begin visiting campuses and interview with college representatives to help you get a real feel for college and campus life. This is especially true whether you commute or live on campus.

September

Register for the October or November SAT and SAT Subject exams. Be sure to check the SAT dates so that you don't miss the deadline. Now is the time to make your final decision on colleges you want to apply to. If you are the student, be sure you have a clear picture of your finances and what debt you will leave college with. Many college students do not have a full understanding of either what their parents will owe, or what they will owe for student loans.

Research what criteria homeschoolers need to meet at your chosen school. Are there extra portfolios or essay submissions required? If so, gather those items now and begin to arrange them in a professional looking portfolio. Some schools will accept electronic transmissions of work, and others will want to see the actual work when you visit.

Now is also the time to follow up on those requested letters of recommendation, especially if you are applying early. Some colleges want letters of recommendation submitted directly to the college and others will allow homeschoolers to mail or email them in. Homeschoolers can ask their employers, a teacher from a class they took, or a minister or Director of Religious Education for letters of recommendation. Even if those you asked for a letter submit it directly to the school, be sure to get a copy for your own records and for future application processes.

By now you should have created an account for The Common Application if the colleges you've selected use it. It is best to check in on the common app at least weekly so you are sure that you are not missing emails, messages or other requirements that are needed.

Staying organized is paramount during the college application process. Create a chart of deadlines for financial aid, forms, portfolios and transcripts. Check off each item on the master list as you move through the process and be sure your student is involved. Pay particular attention to early decision, early action, and preferred application deadlines. Early decision and early action plans can be valuable to students, but only for those who have thought through their college options carefully and have a clear preference for one institution.

Early decision plans are binding and early action plans are nonbinding. A student who is accepted as an early decision applicant, must attend the college and notify all other colleges applied to, of the early decision. Early action plans are nonbinding in that students receive an early response to their application, but do not have to commit to the college until the normal reply date of May 1. Homeschooling parents should make sure that their student understands this key distinction between the two plans. If you have not yet decided on your school or major, it might be best to forgo an early decision or action plan.

College essays should be worked on throughout the entire senior year until submission time. This is one area that I strongly suggest having an outside party — other than the parent, read and evaluate the essay. When Patrick applied to college, I hated his essay. As a writer, I thought he had put little thought into it, and felt it was lacking in critical thinking and staying on topic. I had a former English teacher friend read it for a second opinion and they agreed with my son! I had to step back and realize that while I taught this child for many years, I was very much wrong in this instance. Do not put off writing your essay until the last minute. Revise constantly and ask for help in evaluating the writing if you need to.

###

October

Fall is the time to continue to research schools to narrow your list down to roughly six to eight schools. By this time, you should have a clear idea of which schools suit your needs. Take advantage of college fairs and virtual tours to explore the schools. Virtual tours are great if you cannot attend the campus visitor day. Sometimes, they include information on areas of campus or clubs, that are not included in physical tours, that may be of interest to you.

Complete your applications if you are applying for early decision or early action, they are due by November. Begin researching scholarships and grants. Does your parent's employer offer college scholarships to employee's children? Is there a scholarship available based on your volunteer work or hours? Are there scholarships available in your chosen major? Go after each and every scholarship available because every penny counts when trying to whittle down that college debt burden.

Make sure you are checking your transcript for accuracy on a regular basis. Keep track of all application components and deadlines: applications, test scores, letters of recommendation, and financial aid materials. An incomplete application will delay/impact your chances for admission.

Out of the Box Learning

###

November

The fall SAT's are really your last chance to retake this test and improve your grade if you feel it can be better. Don't let your grades slide during your senior year. It's easy to be distracted from school work when working on applications or other teen oriented things. Not paying attention to your studies and GPA can be disastrous for your admissions chances.

Make sure you've submitted all components of your applications if you are applying to colleges with November deadlines for early decision, or preferred application. Put the final touches on your application essays and have someone give it a final edit.

###

December — January

Despite the holiday rush and New Year's, it's time to complete your applications for regular admissions. Don't let this critical time slip through your fingers by not staying on top of your applications. Make sure you've had your test scores sent to all colleges that require them, and confirm that your letters of recommendation have been sent from those you asked.

Contact colleges that didn't send you a confirmation receipt for your application, to be sure everything is in order and submit the FAFSA — Free Application for Student Financial Aid. You can save time and effort if you download the IRS data retrieval tool. It will transfer your income tax data directly from the IRS to your online FAFSA form.

If you are accepted to a school through early decision, be sure to follow directions carefully. Submit required forms, and notify the other schools to which you applied of your decision to withdraw from their consideration. This will allow space for another waiting student and seal your decision with the college of your choice.

###

February — March

If you submitted the FAFSA, you should receive the Student Aid Report (SAR). After the information you provided is analyzed, you will receive an SAR that contains all the data you entered on the FAFSA. Review the SAR carefully for errors. The form will highlight the items that may need attention. Follow the directions for making and submitting corrections and submit any corrections immediately, because errors can cost you thousands of dollars in lost funding. Make sure to keep a copy of the SAR for your records.

Students should be reminded to keep their grades high and not slack. Colleges can revoke offers of admission if your grades plummet during senior year. Schools will ask for final grades and transcripts once courses are completed.

Some acceptance letters may start to arrive and it's customary to not get into every single school you applied to. Schools choose students for a variety of reasons, but if you feel you have been overlooked, or should be admitted, call the admissions office to arrange an interview. You might gain some valuable insight on how to conduct yourself better during an interview, or what other things you could have done to make your application more attractive. Don't panic if you don't immediately hear from the colleges; many, many decisions are not mailed out until April.

Out of the Box Learning
###

April

As your days wind down to learning where you might be spending the next four years, keep track of all acceptances, rejections, and waitlists on your master list. If waitlisted, check with the college to see if they have a firm date to let you know of acceptance. Most will not contact a student until they hear from all other students who have been accepted, so it might be best to move ahead with other plans. You can always change your plans if you get off a waitlist or are switched to an accepted student status. Some wait lists move very fast, and others may provide no chance of you being accepted into your choice of college.

If you have ruled out any colleges that accepted you, notify them. This is a courtesy to other applicants, and it will help the colleges manage their waitlists and extend the correct number of acceptance letters. Respond to the accepted student open houses if offered, and prepare a list of questions to bring with you. After you have visited the campuses, narrow your decision down to three or less colleges based on acceptance.

###

May — June

Most schools have a deposit deadline of May 1 for tuition and housing. Don't be late with your payment or you might not have a place to live. If needed, you may be able to request an extension on the deposit based on financial need. Housing costs are usually incorporated into your student loans but many colleges do require a deposit that is not covered. Be sure you have planned for all of these incidentals because they can add up fairly fast. Ask ahead of time for this financial cost, because it can sometimes cost thousands of dollars. If the cost of the deposit is beyond your means, ask the school to adjust your loans to include this. Some colleges automatically do this knowing the cost exceeds what many can afford. Be sure that you notify your college if you receive any scholarships from outside organizations as it will affect the amount of financial aid you receive.

Do not assume private colleges are too expensive. Financial aid at private colleges may be more generous than public colleges. Many public colleges tend to be more financially generous for out of state applicants. Most importantly, become familiar with the financial aid language. Most highschools have financial aid nights that both parent and students can attend for more information or college aid organizations. Make an appointment to speak to someone at the college planning organization to learn more about financial planning and what you might have to contribute to your child's college fund. Assets, estimated family contribution (EFC) and other factors all play a part in what has to be reported and what is considered for your child's financial aid.

Be aware of how outside scholarships can affect your financial aid package. When a school offers a grant, outside scholarships may reduce that grant amount. For example, a $1,000 scholarship from an outside organization may reduce the grant by that total amount or a percentage of the scholarship amount ($500-$1000 less in grant money from the school).

Do not be afraid to ask a college for more money. Many private schools will offer more if they really want you. When my son narrowed his choices down to his top two schools, both had offered the exact same financial aid package. The out of state school had more private funds available compared to the in-state school. I let the out of state school know that they were my son's first choice but financially, it would be a struggle for us. I asked if there was anything more they could do for us, and they offered another $5000 in grants and scholarships to sweeten the package. We accepted!

Out of the Box Learning

We did the same thing during his sophomore year when our family suffered a financial hardship. Tuition costs had gone up during his sophomore year, but we asked again and the school offset that tuition difference again with more funding. Make sure you ask the school for any scholarships that are available as well. Every penny matters and a scholarship of a few hundred dollars will help buy textbooks or other needed supplies. Scholarships may also be available in your child's selected major so be sure to ask about those too. Don't be afraid to ask every single year for more financial help. It just may pay off.

Now is the time to have your final transcripts sent to colleges. Send thank you letters to everyone who helped you in the application process like those who wrote letters of recommendation. Let your mentors and recommenders know the results of your college search.

Graduate. Congratulations!

July — August after Senior Year

Read all mailings from your college carefully. Often, important registration and housing material is sent in the summer. Students sometimes throw this important mail away thinking it junk or advertising when in fact, dorms and housing decisions are being made. Information on registering for your classes will arrive as well.

If you get your housing assignment, take advantage of the summer to get to know your roommate. Figure out who will bring what items. You don't need two TVs and two microwaves in your tiny room, if at all. Many colleges now have kitchenettes for student use and common rooms for watching TV and social gatherings.

Homeschooling parents should prepare for the emotions of sending a child off to college and realize that children may struggle for the first several months, as they adjust to campus life and new independence. Stay in good communication with your student and contact college counselors if you need any assistance in helping your college student to adjust to this new life style.

The process to get your homeschooled child to college is not difficult when you prepare and learn the steps. Be proud of yourself and your child for reaching this wonderful milestone!

Closing

Homeschooling is not a one size fits all model. While my hope is that this book has been helpful and supportive, you must create your own path just as I did. Your path will look far different than my journey.

As a coach and longtime homeschooler, I love that my experiences and my writing help people to see how valuable homeschooling can be. But at the same time, each of wants to be seen as a unique individual, with our very own ambitions and experiences. I want for all children's learning to be celebrated, honored, cherished and individualized. I want all parents to feel empowered to provide an education for their children that is both fulfilling and rewarding.

As a community, homeschoolers want greater understanding and acknowledgment that we too are finding our way. But each and every child, whether homeschooled or attending public school needs to be seen as an individual, not as products of a philosophy or test.

As homeschoolers, may we hold fast to our shared values of honoring children and thinking out of the box. The goal of homeschooling our children should be about nurturing and celebrating each individual, no matter who they are, no matter what path they are on and no matter how long the journey takes.

Those first tentative steps we took all those years ago has left us with the gift of having lived our lives together — as whole family unit. I did not know what a profound impact homeschooling would have on our lives — that so immensely shaped our lives for the better. I did not know that homeschooling would lead me to recognize my own strengths and gifts, and to encourage those same traits in my kids and in others.

Today, I'll gift some used curriculum to another homeschooler and settle into a cup of afternoon coffee on my deck, while my kids grow and find their next learning experience. I am a bystander in their learning, with full trust that they are equipped to succeed and answer the hard questions of the world. Fully trusting their magnificent hearts to make good decisions.

The years have passed for us with both great struggle and with great joy. It has not always been easy, but it has always been blessed and in every experience, a lesson to be learned. Every experience is a stepping stone to something better, something different, and something much more remarkable than the last experience.

I hope you will join us Out of the Box.

Epilogue

A few moments later, he cocked his head slightly and told the doctor about the larvae, pupa and chrysalis stages that led up to the beautiful butterfly and how you shouldn't ever help a butterfly out of its cocoon. In order to grow and survive, it must do this on its own — taking the time to stretch its wings and dry off and stretch again and take a breath. It was only then, after enduring the struggles of bursting forth from the cocoon, that the butterfly could fly away and become what it was meant to be.

***

My butterfly. Patrick is now Pat and has finished sophomore year in college. She has made her transition to a beautiful butterfly. We couldn't be prouder.

About the Author

Beverly Burgess, is passionate about homeschooling and alternative learning. As a Homeschool Coach with over a decade in homeschooling experience, she has helped hundreds of families on their journey to homeschooling. She was the Executive Director of a large nonprofit homeschooling group from 2009-2016, runs an international social media support group for homeschool group leaders, and has been featured in magazine articles and podcasts and with <u>Taming the High Cost of College</u>, and <u>College Funding Resource</u>. She has been a keynote speaker at Homeschooling Through Highschool and Introduction to Homeschooling workshops for the public, and is a fervent advocate for homeschooling rights and law. Bev coaches new and seasoned homeschoolers through all stages of home education, and is an admitted curriculum hoarder.

In her pre-homeschooling life, Bev was a Registered Nurse and held advanced certification in Neurosurgical Intensive Care Nursing, Advanced Cardiac Life Support, Critical Care Nursing, and spent almost twenty years working on the Neurosurgical Intensive Care Unit at a big city hospital. She has contributed to national studies on Tourette's Syndrome and ran a large adoption support group in Rhode Island as well as having served as chairperson for a $2-million-dollar capital campaign for green building initiative. She, her husband of twenty-six years and their three children, ages 12, 17 and 20 live in Rhode Island with an array of animals and big organic vegetable garden. Her oldest is a junior at a small liberal arts college in Vermont and is a writing major.

Contact Bev through her website: http://www.beverlyburgess.com or info@beverlyburgess.com

www.ingramcontent.com/pod-product-compliance
Lightning Source LLC
Chambersburg PA
CBHW051045160426
43193CB00010B/1071